Tank-Fighter Team

Tank-Fighter Team

By
LIEUTENANT ROBERT M. GERARD

(Formerly of the French Armored Force)

COACHWHIP PUBLICATIONS

Landisville, Pennsylvania

Tank-Fighter Team, by Lieutenant Robert M. Gerard
Original publication 1942
Copyright © 2010 Coachwhip Publications
No claim made on public domain material.

ISBN 1-61646-023-7
ISBN-13 978-1-61646-023-5

CoachwhipBooks.com

CONTENTS

FOREWORD

Few personal narratives of the Battle of France have been written by soldiers, especially by French soldiers who tasted to the uttermost the bitter dregs of defeat. And even fewer have been the authentic accounts of how the actual fighting progressed, of the tactics of small units.

On the other hand, there are innumerable reports in print that recount the overwhelming superiority of the modern German Army over "the finest infantry in the world." From these reports the impression has gained wide circulation that France apparently was blind to the significance of aircraft, tanks, armored trucks and motorcycles in modern war. The truth is France had all of these but her tragedy is that she had too few and too often didn't know how to use them to best advantage.

The French mechanized units fought valiantly and oftentimes successfully against overwhelming odds, as they attempted to stave off the Nazi sweep across the Lowlands and northern France. Such a unit was the Groupe Franc of which Lieutenant Gerard was second in command. In numerous engagements his Groupe repulsed and held back the advancing Nazis while the body of the French Army retreated from one position to another, never making the final stand which France and the whole world (including the enemy) awaited.

Lieutenant Gerard tells the story of the actions in which his Groupe participated, of how it maneuvered and how it fought. The dogged, indomitable, persistently intelligent leadership of the captain commanding the Groupe stands forth as a splendid example of initiative and endurance for all leaders of fighting men. And Lieutenant Gerard himself reveals such qualities of resourcefulness and aggressiveness as to make his story one that the American soldier, whether he fights in a tank or otherwise, can study with profit. The picture of cooperation he gives between the differing units of a fighting combat team is particularly valuable.

Lieutenant Gerard was in America attending Harvard University Business School under an American Field Service Fellowship when the war broke out in September, 1939. In November, two days after he had married an American girl, he was called back to France for military duty. Accompanied by his bride he returned to his homeland and attended the Saumur Military Academy, specializing in tanks. He volunteered to serve with the Groupe Franc. After France gave up he escaped to the United States and has taken steps to become an American citizen.

Tank-Fighter Team is more than a picture of a "suicide" unit in action against overwhelming odds. In it are many lessons for the American soldier as he prepares to fight the same enemy and the Far Eastern enemy, who uses many similar methods of war to those of the foe in Europe.

The Editors,
The Infantry Journal.

I: Abbeville to Rouen

In November, 1939, I was called back to France for military duty and left the United States on a French convoy. When I completed my course at the Saumur Cavalry School, I was given a commission as second lieutenant in the French Armored Force. I was retained for a few weeks at the School to get additional training in tank engineering. On May 17, 1940, I was transferred to the organization center of the French Armored Force in Monthlery, twenty miles south of Paris. There I waited for my assignment to a fighting unit, and finally, I learned that the French were building up several armored combat teams.

We were told that these new units would be sent on dangerous missions and that everyone who joined them must be a volunteer. I volunteered and was fortunate enough to be given the best possible job in my particular team, the job of second-in-command, under the captain in command. And so on May 26th I was assigned to one of the "Groupes Franc" formed in those last desperate days. Groupe Franc means unattached group: we could be sent anywhere we were needed to aid hard-pressed troops. We were to operate directly under the headquarters of any infantry division which could use our services.

The specific mission of our Groupe Franc was one of rear-guard action—to protect the retreat of an infantry division. We were actually a special antitank unit, protecting the division against tank attacks. That the group was pretty much of a "suicide unit" is apparent from the fact that out of 250 men in the group, over 100 were killed, 50 were wounded, 80 were taken prisoner, and only 17 came back.

The composition of this combat team has particular interest because it included, within a small unit and under the unified command of a captain, five medium tanks, five armored cars, two 25-mm. antitank guns, two 47-mm. antitank guns, fifty infantrymen on trucks with heavy machine guns, twenty-five sidecars with machine guns, ten solo motorcycles with machine guns for reconnaissance, liaison, and transmission of orders, several ammunition and supply trucks, three gasoline trucks, one kitchen truck, one repair truck, one telephone truck, and one radio truck. It was thus a little army in itself, an integrated combat team. A more detailed description of the composition of the unit is given in the first table in the Appendix.

The equipment of our Groupe Franc was brand new. It took us from May 26th to June 3d to get fully equipped and ready to leave for the front. The medium tanks were the French Somua, model 1939, which the Germans have said was the best tank in the Battle of France. (In fact, I have heard they are making them now.) The armored cars were Panhard cars. The antitank guns were of the two newest models in the French Army, towed by brand-new six-wheel prime-movers of the Laffly type. The sidecars were Indian machines, made in Springfield, Massachusetts. The solo motorcycles were Royals, built in England. The command cars used by the officers were small French passenger cars, the Peugeot 302. Finally, most of the supply and ammunition trucks, and the trucks used to carry the fifty infantrymen, were General Motors trucks. Practically every man in the Groupe Franc carried a rifle, Model 1936. A more detailed description of the equipment is given in the second table in the Appendix.

Not only were the officers in the Groupe Franc volunteers, but the men too. About half of them were Foreign Legion men. They were extremely hard to handle away from battle, but they proved to be remarkable fighters in battle itself. About one-fourth of them were regulars, and the rest draftees. The draftees, however, had gone through two years of military training and had been recalled by the French Army for the war.

My captain, in command of the Groupe Franc, was a regular army officer, thirty-five years old. He had served for years in the motorized cavalry and had seen actual battle experience in Belgium in the present war as a commander of a company of armored cars. All his armored cars had been destroyed in combat, a few in one fight and a few in another, until he finally found himself surrounded by the Germans around Cambrai, in the northern part of France. With his last three armored cars he broke through a German motorized infantry column and managed to rejoin the French forces. The fact that our captain had already been through it gave us confidence in him as commander. It was mainly through his remarkable leadership that our Groupe Franc accomplished its missions swiftly and efficiently.

Now that the mission, composition, and equipment have been described, I can attempt to tell what the Groupe Franc did during the Battle of France. There are, however, many limitations which must be borne in mind. The first limitation is my memory which is by no means perfect.

I intend to tell only of what I saw myself. Since I am not an expert in military matters, I cannot embark on problems of high strategy and tactics. I will not be able to present the whole picture. Our unit was a small one. And what I saw was

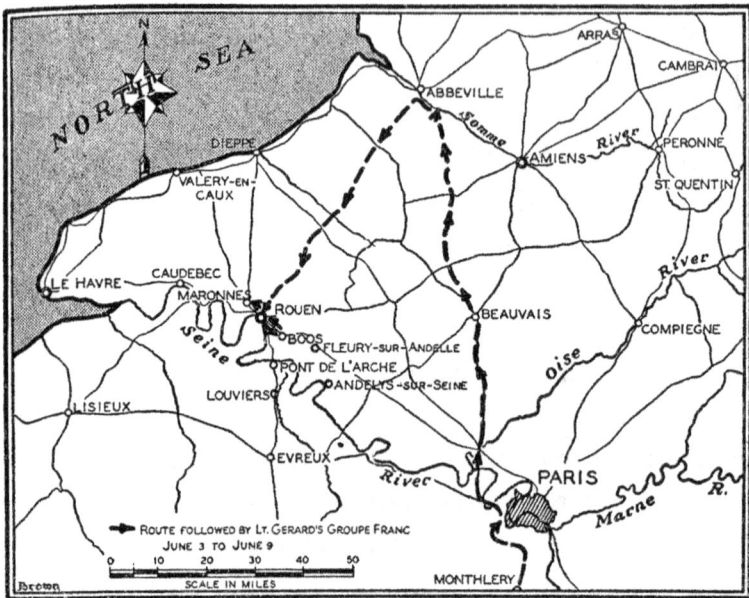

Map 1

what the second-in-command of such a unit can see—which is a very limited part of the whole big battle. Another limitation is simply that, as every one knows, we did not have a very long time to fight, for the collapse of France came suddenly.

The small section of the front where our unit fought was the most western flank of the French Army. On this part of the front the Germans did not attack as heavily as they did in the center. What I saw was rear-guard action, a lot of skirmishes between our unit and German advance-guard units. Many, many gaps existed in our line. In fact there was no line. This, with disorganization of the French troops and the complete air superiority of the Germans, led them to use reckless tactics which they probably would not adopt in a different situation. In France there are lots of roads and villages, and the Germans advanced mainly along the roads. Hence I saw very little of open warfare in the full sense. This situation would hardly repeat itself if, for example, the Germans tried to invade this country. In the United States villages and farms are far apart and we have fewer roads per square mile than in France. And so what I shall tell about should be taken as what the Germans did under a certain set of conditions, and we should not jump at conclusions and assume that they would attack the same way under any set of conditions. It is dangerous to make such assumptions about any energetic enemy.

On June 3d, late at night, our unit left for the front. About 10:00 o'clock the next night we reached the Somme River, a little east of Abbeville (map 1). The enemy was supposedly on the other side of it, a few miles to the north. We learned that on a front of thirty miles there were only two brigades of *dragons portés* (motorized infantry) to hold the front. Ordinarily that strength should have been assigned to no more than five miles.

The Germans attacked on June 5th. We were first subjected to a terrific bombardment by German dive-bombers lasting several hours, wave after wave. We lost several men, but not as many as we thought. Later, for nearly an hour, we came under artillery fire from the other side of the Somme, 88-mm. artillery fire that kept pounding and pounding continually. But the French artillery answered. I stayed all that time in a small shell-hole, observing the other side from time to time to see if the Germans were coming. But no sign of them. The artillery shelling killed more and wounded more of us than the Stukas had.

Around the middle of the afternoon, and for no reason at all that I could understand, our unit got the order to retreat at once. Apparently we were the only unit nearby which got this order. When a company of motorized infantry arrived to relieve us, we left the place. We were instructed to go straight south to Rouen, a big industrial city of more than 100,000 inhabitants on the Seine River. There we were to be at the disposal of the general commanding the corps area.

We arrived in Rouen during the morning of June 6th, where we found things in a frightful mess. The bulk of the French Army, except the few troops left along the Somme, appeared to be withdrawing to the south. What I could not understand was that no defense of the Seine had been prepared and that none of the troops moving south were ordered to stop behind that river. They were all going farther to the south, except for our own unit and a neighboring Groupe Franc, which we heard was in position at Pont de l'Arche, along the Seine.

At noon on June 7th, our Groupe Franc was assigned to defend Boos, a village on the north side of the Seine about six miles southeast of Rouen (map 2). We were to stay there until the order came to retreat. The other Groupe Franc was to be sent to Igoville about twelve miles south of Rouen. Our order indicated that a German panzer division had broken through the French lines on the Somme, and that a mechanized column was heading toward Les-Andelys-sur-Seine, twenty miles southeast of Rouen, and would probably attack Rouen from the southeast. That is why we were sent to Boos, southeast of Rouen. There was to be no supporting artillery to help us, and probably no air force.

We arrived in Boos late in the afternoon of June 7th. Our job there was to establish what is called a *bouchon* (a cork), a French military term, which means a strong point for the defense of a vital road. The defense of this village we then set about organizing in the same manner in which we organized other villages later on. I generally went ahead of our main column in a sidecar to prepare in advance an outline of our defense dispositions. The first thing I would always do upon arriving in a village would be to find the places where

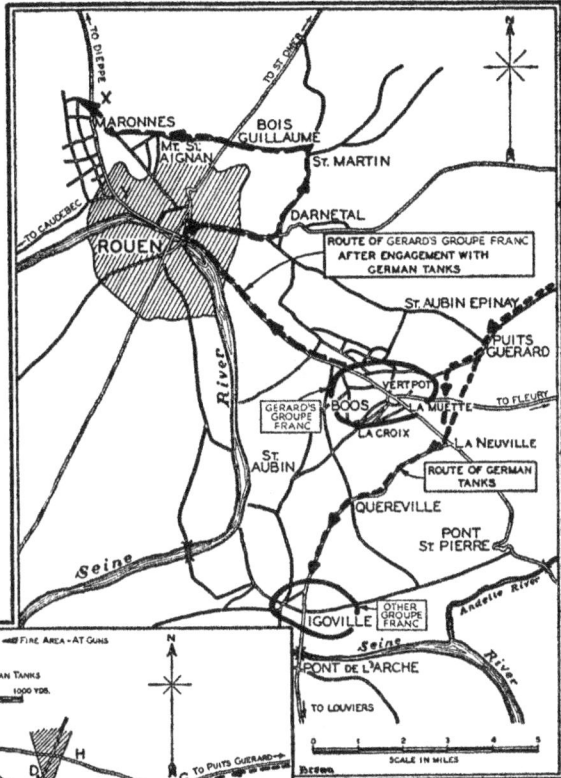

Map 3

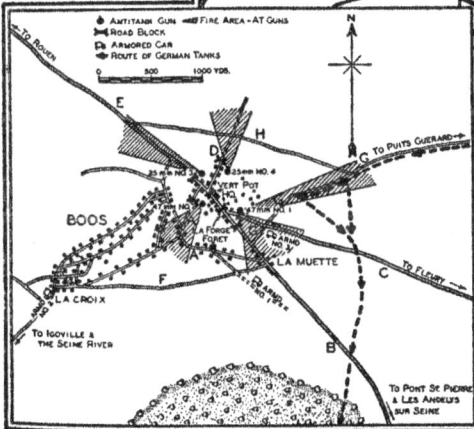

Map 2

our vehicles could be camouflaged or hidden so as not to be visible from the air. My captain had learned from bitter experience in Belgium that the trees in the central square of a town or a village always attracted Stukas. At Boos, therefore, I looked for several orchards where the vehicles could be placed under the trees far enough apart (at least twenty to thirty yards), so that the same bomb would not damage more than one vehicle. The radio truck, the telephone truck, and the captain's car were placed in a private garage or a building near a farm chosen as the headquarters for our unit. In the defense of some villages, later in the campaign, I put all the vehicles, except the combat vehicles and the radio truck, in a wood or some inconspicuous place off the roads a few miles to the south of the village we were to defend.

Camouflage and concealment from the air were my first thought. I had learned their importance fast enough after being bombed a few times. In order to prevent the vehicles from jamming up in the streets of the village, I prepared a simple sketch to show where each vehicle should be hidden. When the column arrived in the village, I gave a copy of this sketch to each platoon commander. Five minutes at the most after the column arrived in a village, not a single vehicle could be seen from the air.

The second thing to take care of, as soon as the column arrived in a village, was protection from tank attack. We would lose no time in sending one tank out each road converging on the village, from 200 yards to half a mile out from the outskirts. And within a few minutes, we would unhook our antitank guns from their prime-movers and place them on the different roads in temporary emplacement until we could prepare a better.

After this, I generally went around the village with my captain to help him devise a more permanent and complete defense. Thinking primarily of tank attack, we sought first the best places to put our antitank guns. Once that was done, we could then build the rest of the defense around those guns.

Boos, we found, was a difficult place to defend with the limited means we had. As the map shows, the village had many streets and there were many roads converging toward it, and we had only four antitank guns. The only friendly troops in the area we knew of were the other Groupe Franc in Igoville, and a few infantry troops at Bois Guillaume and Mt. St. Aignan, north of Rouen. For us to establish a continuous line of defense in contact with those elements was impossible. All we could expect to do was to place a few strong points on vital roads. To try to defend all the thickly settled area from Vert Pot to La Croix, which was Boos proper, would be useless and dangerous. The multiplicity of roads would permit the Germans to split our Groupe Franc in small sections and take us from the rear. We decided therefore to concentrate our defense in the area between Vert Pot and La Forge Forêt.

We used the two 47-mm. antitank guns to defend the southeast outskirts of the village. This was the direction from which the Germans would probably attack if they came from Les Andelys. We used the two 25-mm. antitank guns to defend the roads that led toward Rouen, along which the Germans were less likely to attack. Thus our antitank defense was set up in all directions because experience had taught our commander that the Germans were apt to appear from unexpected directions.

To our antitank guns we gave roads to defend as the principal missions because the roads were of course the only passage German tanks could follow in breaking through the village. The houses of the village were all old stone houses, and were very close together, almost touching each other. It had been my captain's experience during the Battle of Belgium that German tanks rarely advanced in waves except when under antitank fire or when they were attacking a stabilized front with extensively organized defenses. As far as I am concerned, I never saw hundreds of German tanks rolling wave after wave across the country, sweeping everything before them. Every time I saw a German force advancing, it simply consisted of a small mechanized column on a road.

As for the detailed placement of the antitank guns, one 47-mm. antitank gun (1) in Boos, was protecting roads B, C, and G, another (2) was protecting road A. The two 25-mm. antitank guns (3 and 4) were protecting roads E and D, one on each road. The actual emplacements were carefully chosen. For AT gun (1), for instance, we found a place 50 yards north of road C from which the observation on roads B, C, and G was excellent. We put in the gun behind the wall of a garden and made a hole in the wall, which gave added protection for the crew against machine-gun fire from German tanks.

At any time we avoided putting our antitank guns directly in the axis of the road, because they would be discovered too quickly. At Boos we dug our antitank guns into the ground. At several other places, however, the Germans gave us no time to prepare good emplacements.

We installed strong roadblocks on all the streets converging toward the center of our defense. The extent to which we were able to build effective roadblocks depended on the time we had before an attack came, and upon the fatigue of our troops. We never received any help from the French engineers in building our roadblocks. At Boos we had the time to prepare roadblocks that were good and strong. We found many agricultural implements nearby, such as tractors, harrows, and carts, and piled them up. We fastened them together with strong cables; we cut trees and piled them on top of all the farm implements. A roadblock has to be pretty high otherwise tanks just go right through it. But sometimes, when there was not much time to prepare them, we used just two or three abandoned trucks to make a roadblock.

In defending a village, we built our roadblocks on the streets at points where houses were on both sides, so that the tanks would not be able to get around them. Where this could not be done, we would try to coordinate our roadblocks with mines placed to each side of it, so that a German tank trying to detour the roadblock would hit them.

Of course, we also coordinated our roadblocks with our antitank defense. We tried always to place them in such a way that German tanks would see them only at the last moment. At Boos, for example, for our 47-mm. at (2) we placed the roadblock behind a curve of the road. When a German tank or armored car first saw it suddenly there would be at least a second or two of hesitation on the part of the tank crew. Our antitank crew would take advantage of these seconds to open fire at top speed. For this to be done successfully, the antitank gun had to be placed to one side of the roadblock so that the crew could see the enemy tank well and fire at it accurately. While the crew waited for the enemy it kept the gun aimed always at the exact point where the German tank crew would hesitate as it came against the block. The primary mission of the antitank gun was to watch that point. Secondary targets were given to the gun crew on both sides of this point.

When we would get both the roadblocks and antitank-gun emplacements finally set up to our satisfaction, our tanks would come back to the center of the village and we would camouflage them at once, and hold them as a reserve in case of an attack. At Boos, when our tanks thus came back, we kept two of our armored cars as a reserve and sent the other three out on the roads B and C, and to La Croix. These armored cars were our warning system against the enemy's tanks. They went out on their roads beyond the field of vision of the antitank-gun crew, and watched for approaching enemy forces from some good observation point a little off the main road. The cars would keep constantly in touch by radio with the Groupe Franc command post in the big farm in the middle of our defense area.

Near its emplacement each antitank-gun crew had a light machine gun for its protection if the enemy decided to storm the antitank-gun emplacement with motorized infantry. Hence in the defense of Boos, the four roads could all be taken under machine-gun fire. For this reason, we did not use any of our motorized infantry to defend the roads.

We chose the emplacement of the six heavy machine guns of the motorized infantry platoon in such a way that their fire would cover the areas not defended by the light machine guns of the antitank-gun platoons. Here again it was of the utmost importance to defend the village from all sides. We put several of the machine guns in the back gardens or orchards around the village, preparing at once a good emplacement for each of them. We had time to do that, however, at only two other places. We put one or two machine guns in houses, in the event of street fighting following a break through our antitank defense by the German tanks. Our motorized infantry had armor-piercing bullets (caliber .30 and .50 for the light and heavy machine guns) effective against unarmored vehicles and armored cars at close range.

It took us all the evening and night of June 7th to set up an adequate defense of Boos. And when, by morning, the job was done, we sent the men to rest, leaving only one or two at each gun.

The two armored cars in reserve and the motorcycle platoon had had a good night's rest. My captain and I decided we should use them. We sent out two patrols, each of an armored car and one motorcycle squad (5 sidecars) following the car. The first patrol went in the direction of Puits Guerard, keeping in touch with us all the time by radio; it swung south to Fleury-sur-Andelle and came back around noon. Not a single enemy vehicle in sight, it reported.

The second patrol went to Pont St. Pierre to observe for one hour along the banks of the Andelle River. Then it went west toward Igoville, where it effected liaison with the other Groupe Franc. The patrol came back to Boos through Quereville and La Neuville, and arrived there around 1:00 in the afternoon. It had seen no enemy vehicle. This second patrol, however, did bring in some information. Refugees seen at Pont St. Pierre all agreed that Germans were approaching Les Andelys from the north and were expected there any minute. All French troops had left Les Andelys and crossed the Seine. Apparently there, as in Rouen, the troops were not stopped and reorganized behind the Seine, but were retreating farther to the south. We now became convinced that the Seine would not be defended, except by a few rear-guard units like our own. We radioed this information at once to corps headquarters.

When the two armored cars came back to Boos, they were sent to relieve two of the three armored cars that had been observing all night and all morning on the roads around the village. This matter of relieving men and making them take turns is very important in keeping any unit in fighting spirit and condition. Later on in the Battle of France so much of our matériel had been destroyed and we had so few men left when the enemy gave us no chance to rest—which was practically all the time—no such relief could be provided. For this reason many of our men, especially the officers, did not sleep for several days, and were fighting in a sort of dream. The Germans, on the other hand, had plenty of fresh troops for relief.

After the patrols came back, on that afternoon of June 8th, everything was quiet in Boos. Most of our men were asleep, with only a few on duty at the antitank guns and machine guns. We saw several German planes during the afternoon, but none of them attacked us. Around 3:00, an observation plane circled rather low over our village. We did not move or fire, in order not to reveal our presence.

At 4:00 P.M., a French colonel presented himself to my captain. He showed a regular identification card and said he had been sent from corps headquarters to tell us that at around 4:30 or 5:00 P.M. fourteen French tanks would arrive on their way south to defend Rouen, and that we should not fire at them. The tanks could be recognized by the fact that their turrets would be open and that white flags would be waved by the crew of each tank.

We had never seen this colonel before. It was very peculiar that corps headquarters had not sent us the message by radio. And so at once we sent a message asking for confirmation. The officer in charge said he knew nothing about it. In view of all this, my captain ordered me to have all men awakened and placed at their combat posts. I sent messages warning the three armored cars on the outskirts of the village and likewise had the tank crews prepared. Finally, I arranged to have a noncommissioned officer meet the commander of the tanks as soon as they were sighted.

A little after 4:30, the 47-mm. antitank-gun crew at (1) reported by telephone that it had seen armored vehicles in the distance along road G—the road to Puits Guerard on which no armored car had been stationed. The other AT guns, which had been connected with the command post by telephone were at once warned.

The tanks were now slowly approaching. With my field glasses I could see them in the distance with their turrets open and the white flags waving. I now ordered the noncommissioned officer to meet the commander of the tanks. The noncom jumped on a solo motorcycle and rode out toward them. Just as he got about halfway out to them from our anti-tank gun he suddenly turned on the road and headed back at full speed. Obviously something was wrong. Then, as suddenly, I saw the white flags disappear, the turrets close. The leading tank opened fire at the noncom who fell from his motorcycle hit. They were unquestionably German tanks, and the French officer had been nothing but a German spy or a fifth columnist.

Immediately my captain was informed of the situation. I stayed not far from the 47-mm. at (1), from which I could have a good view of what was going on and inform my captain accordingly. I watched the tanks come down the road toward us. They were German mediums (22 tons, with a 77-mm. antitank gun). There were just 14 tanks—no reconnaissance, no armored cars, no motorcycles. Maybe there was motorized infantry following, but I could not see it. Recognizing the tanks as mediums, I immediately gave the order to send a message to the armored cars to retreat at once into the village.

The captain had a message sent to corps headquarters to the effect that we were being attacked by 14 tanks coming from Puits Guerard. The captain suggested that corps headquarters get in touch with the other Groupe Franc by radio, for we had been out of touch with them, and ask whether the tanks of the other Groupe Franc couldn't come toward Boos and effect a surprise attack from the south. The general did not like the idea of sending the tanks of the other Groupe Franc so many miles to the north.

Apparently he was still thinking of World War I where eight to ten miles was a long distance, but in this war of movement such a distance was negligible. Besides, the use of tanks in small numbers, easily destroyed piecemeal by the enemy, was typical of the attitude and tactics of many French staff officers.

My captain decided to cut red tape and send one liaison man full speed to Igoville on a solo motorcycle to ask the captain commanding the other Groupe Franc for support. We had apparently made a big mistake when we had counted on a smooth radio liaison with the other Groupe Franc through corps headquarters. We should have established direct radio contact ourselves.

When the first German tank came close enough, approximately 800 yards, the 47-mm. antitank-gun crew opened fire. At this position I had placed the crew I considered most efficient, because antitank gun (1) was the most important spot in our defense. This crew really knew how to fire. In two shots it hit the first German tank in the column and put it out of action. The shell seemed to have gone through the tank like butter. But our feeling of complacency over this did not last long. The second tank was shooting high-explosive shell against the edges of the village. One of the shells fell not very far away. The 47-mm. antitank-gun crew, however, opened fire again and got this second tank. The German column then hesitated a little. I crawled to the telephone and reported to my captain, who told me that he was sending the tanks out now to counterattack, and for the antitank-gun crew to take care not to shoot at them.

I could hear the rumbling of our tanks leaving Boos as I talked. My captain said he had ordered three tanks to leave on road A and pass by the church, to meet the front of the German tank column around La Muette. Our other two tanks were leaving on road D, and were to turn right on road H, and surprise the German column from the rear. It was a pincers movement on a small scale.

The three next German tanks in the column kept on the road, passed the two disabled tanks, and headed full speed toward road C, their machine guns firing at us during their movement. I had been well advised to put this antitank gun behind the thick stone wall, as I had, because bullets were now hitting the wall. Even so, one man of the gun crew was soon slightly wounded. I signalled by hand to three infantry-men to take him to the rear.

The antitank gun kept firing and hit the last of three tanks heading toward road C. This was the third in the space of a few minutes. Next, the two other tanks left the road and headed toward the six German tanks that had left the road before. Then when they joined, the whole group of eight tanks headed toward road C across the fields. Obviously the Germans had decided not to attack us directly. Their movement could have two purposes; either to avoid combat entirely or to go around the village and test our defense from the rear.

I could not see the rest of the German column. Perhaps those tanks were enveloping us on road H. If that were so, our two tanks sent there could take care of them. The antitank gun fired at the six tanks going across the field, but with little success for the range was long and they were far apart from each other, and now kept zigzagging all the time. But they continued to fire back at us with high-explosive shells, one of which came pretty near and cut the telephone line. From then on I had to use messengers to keep in touch with my captain.

What happened next happened quickly, and was confus-ing. The German tanks, still in the fields, crossed road C and were now heading south toward road B. Just after getting across road C one of them was hit by our antitank gun. That makes four, I thought; only ten more to go. Then, with aston-ishment, I saw armored car No. 1 cross road B, and move to the north as if to have a crack at the German tanks. The car commander must be crazy, I thought, and he is not following orders to retreat to the village.

About this time I suddenly heard gun fire over on our left to the north of us. It must be our two tanks meeting the three

last German tanks in the column. Later, the commander of
one of our tanks told me that they found three German tanks
waiting near road G, which were surprised to see French tanks
coming from their rear. Our tanks destroyed one of the enemy
tanks, and the other tanks left. And those must have been
the two German tanks I saw next in the distance leaving road
G and heading toward the south across the fields at full speed,
in the same direction as the other tanks. These tanks were
too far off to fire at.

Apparently the "crazy" armored-car commander was firing
at the German tanks, but without any success, and the Germans were firing back at the car. Then our three French tanks
crossed road B at full speed in the hamlet of La Muette, left
the road for the field northeast of the hamlet, and headed
right toward the German tanks. The lieutenant commanding
the 47-mm. antitank gun had to order his gun to cease firing
for fear of hitting our own tanks. The German tanks were
approximately 1,000 yards from the gun. As soon as they saw
the French tanks, they stopped firing at us with their high-
explosive shells which was a real relief as far as we were concerned because they had spotted the antitank gun and by now
were firing accurately. For the last few minutes, the antitank-
gun crew had found it more and more difficult to fire, because we had to lie flat in the small foxholes we had dug the
day before to avoid the shell fire. This fire killed one man of
the gun crew.

Now the German and French tanks were having a hot fight
of it and making a terrific noise. We were outnumbered, but
had the advantage of surprise. During the second or so that the
Germans took to swing their turrets around, I think that one
German tank was hit. I say "I think," because it is hard to
imagine how fast and confused a small action like this one is.

As they fought, the German tanks still kept moving toward the south. Evidently they had no intention of attacking

Boos, and their mission, I assumed, was to reach the Seine at some point unknown to us. Shortly the six remaining German tanks were all heading south at full speed. They crossed road B with the three French tanks pursuing them and stopping from time to time to fire. The last one of the German tanks was now apparently hit, because it suddenly stopped and did not move any more. At the same moment, I could distinctly see a direct hit on the French tank in the lead, for it stopped, its men probably injured inside or killed.

Meanwhile my captain had left the command post and had joined me to watch the tank battle. He sent a runner to tell the radio operator to send a message to the tanks ordering them to come back to the village. By now the German tanks were heading toward the woods south of Boos where they would probably reorganize their column and continue toward the south and the Seine. It seemed unlikely that they would attack again, for they had taken quite a beating. Our mission to prevent the Germans from crossing through the village toward Rouen had been accomplished thus far. But new columns of enemy tanks might soon be coming at us again, and so it was better to call in the tanks as a reserve ready to strike again in any direction.

Our losses had been small compared to those of the enemy. As well as we could make out, the Germans had lost seven tanks out of their column of fourteen. We had lost one. That tank had been hit so badly that we were almost sure that the crew had been killed. The armored car could also be considered lost, for all attempts to reach its commander by radio had failed, and none of us had seen the armored car since. In Boos itself, we had four men wounded and three killed by machine-gun bullets and high-explosive shells from the German tanks. I had sent the wounded at once by truck to the military hospital in Rouen. With such losses, we could hardly say that we had been victorious. And I wonder whether the action would have ended as well for us if the enemy had been under orders to crush our defense. But the psychological effect on our men of having been able to repulse a tank attack of any size was enormous. A radio message was sent to headquarters indicating the end of the action. Headquarters said the other Groupe Franc would be warned that seven German tanks were heading in their direction. I learned later from an officer of that Groupe that they had destroyed the seven German tanks when they reached Igoville.

About 5:00 o'clock, half a dozen Stukas suddenly came headlong toward us. They machine-gunned us very little at that time, but concentrated on bombing. We had put up camouflage nets over each antitank gun, and their emplacements could not be found from the air. The bombing kept on for a few minutes, but nothing as thorough as the bombing we had received on the south of the Somme River. It set afire one of our trucks, and wounded one more man. We kept firing with our machine guns against the low-flying planes, but brought none of them down. In fact, not once during all the campaign did any of our machine guns shoot down a single plane.

A few minutes after the bombing stopped, we received a message from corps headquarters ordering our Groupe Franc to move at once to Rouen, and then to the suburb of Maronnes. Information gathered by G-2 at corps headquarters was to the effect that the German column had not taken Les Andelys but had crossed the Andelle River somewhat northeast of Boos and was heading directly toward Rouen from the northeast. Infantrymen were defending the woods on the north side of Rouen, but no unit was available to defend the left flank around Maronnes. Some infantry troops would be sent to Boos to take over our position, but we were to move at once. We left within thirty minutes, leaving one truck and four men behind to look for any men who might be still alive in the destroyed tanks, and bring them to the medical corps station in Rouen.

When our unit crossed through Rouen, we found a terrific traffic jam along the banks of the Seine. It was practically impossible to move anywhere near the two bridges over the Seine. But the jam had been caused by an order from corps to close the two bridges to any except military traffic. The captain in charge of the bridge was following the order literally. A long column of refugees in cars was at the approach to the bridge, but he wouldn't let these people cross it. It was against orders. And so the long column of military trucks behind the cars of the refugees could not cross either.

We decided to turn and get to Maronnes by making a wide swing through Darnetal, St. Martin, Bois Guillaume, and Mt. St. Alignan. Nowhere did we see any real defense organized. We met a few English who were manning antiaircraft guns north of Rouen. And when we reached Maronnes, it was getting late, for we had lost nearly two hours in Rouen.

Maronnes was an impossible place to defend adequately with our limited means. On the right we did have protection against tank attack from the slopes, woods, and houses along the main street, and not a single street led toward us from that side. But on the left there were at least a dozen along which the enemy could come and cut the Groupe Franc in several parts. We put a 47-mm. antitank gun at the fork north of Maronnes (map 3) on the road to Dieppe (point X), and another 47-mm. antitank gun at the big fork south of Maronnes at the entrance of Rouen on the road to Caudebec (point Y). We were lucky to find there a prepared roadblock and a prepared emplacement for a 75-mm. gun which our 47-mm. could use. No trace, of course, of the 75; it too had retreated to the south in the general movement.

We put our two 25-mm. antitank guns on two roads between point X and point Y. As far as the other roads were concerned, we just had to hope that German tanks would not use them. We had only machine guns with armor-piercing bullets to defend them.

I spent the night in a sidecar, going back and forth between X and Y, supervising the work done on road blocks and gun emplacements. The men worked on through the night at them. Around 3:00 in the morning of June 9th, a green and then a red rocket was suddenly seen by the crew of the anti-tank gun X. The rockets seemed to come from the woods north of Maronnes. Whether the enemy was there or not, we did not know. A few minutes later we heard the firing of guns in the distance, seemingly coming from the southeast. Could it be that some German force had already gone through Boos and was heading toward Rouen from the southeast? We did not know that, either. Neither did corps headquarters, with which we kept in touch by radio. This uncertainty was hard to take. Yet we could be sure of one thing: we would have to fight again against what odds we did not know. We knew nothing. We were left alone, and we felt alone and without much hope.

II: The Battle of Rouen

When the light of the Sunday of June 9th began to show itself, our Groupe Franc was still in the suburb of Maronnes, prepared to receive the enemy with its machine guns and antitank guns. Early that day a motorcycle patrol and two armored cars were sent northeast to Mt. St. Aignan (see map 4), in order to effect a better liaison with the infantry troops and the British antiaircraft batteries we had seen there the day before. After an hour the patrol came back, reporting that all Allied troops had left during the night without our knowing anything about it. In fact, the patrol had seen a few German motorcyclists there.

We then tried to get in touch with division headquarters, for we wanted to know whether we should still try to defend Maronnes with our right flank exposed. The radio at the division CP made no answer. Accordingly, my captain ordered me to go by motorcycle to the CP, which was on the south side of the Seine, in Rouen itself. At the bridge I left the motorcycle to cross on foot. But first I had to lose fifteen minutes arguing with a captain who would not let me over without an official pass. In the middle of the most tremendous rout in the history of France, the average Frenchman still continued the routine of asking for papers, slips, requisitions. When I reached headquarters I found the place empty. But an orderly there said that headquarters had just been moved to the south but exactly where he did not know.

I went back to the bridge and found there a colonel from headquarters whom I had met before. He said that he had been charged by the division commander to organize the defense of the two Rouen bridges. The Groupe Franc, he said, must now move by echelons toward the bridges.

When my captain heard this he decided that we should try to get all our vehicles across to the south side of the Seine, and defend Rouen from that side. The Seine is an excellent antitank obstacle, 400 yards wide in many places.

But our first hard job was to convince the colonel that this was the best way to use our small "suicide" combat team, and a second big problem was to end the traffic jam which was banked up against the closed bridge; this had to be done if our tanks and armored cars and trucks were to get across. I found that the colonel had a much different plan. His idea was for us to use our tanks to defend the Seine by operating on its north bank—the German bank. I suggested tactfully that in general the defense of a stream was generally made behind it, especially when the defending force is weak. But the colonel decided otherwise; we must defend in front of the bridges. The only thing he approved was the idea of getting all our non-combatant units and the supply, ammunition, kitchen, and radio trucks across the river. This discussion took half an hour at least, and the defense preparations were still to be started. I came back to my unit and we began our movement back toward the bridges, keeping our tanks and armored cars to our rear flank to protect us against tank attack during the movement.

Then I spent another half hour arguing with both the colonel and the captain in charge of the bridges to let us have both bridges opened to traffic so that we could get across as soon as possible. Finally they agreed. It made me almost desperate to see such slowness in arriving at any decision when time saved meant life or death. It took one more hour for the traffic to flow on and over the bridges, until it was the turn of the Groupe Franc to cross. The captain in charge of the bridges only slowed things up further by trying to insist that our military vehicles be allowed to cross first, for there was practically a solid block of refugee cars ahead of us.

The colonel also decided to put two of the four armored cars we still had left on the Pont Cormeille, the east bridge, as fixed forts! Moreover, he had a tank stay in place on the French side near the end of the bridge. This tank was in such a position that it could not even fire across the length of the bridge into the long Street that led from the bridge to the north without great risk of hitting the armored cars or the antitank-gun crew at the north end of the bridge. And when the tank commander tried to move his tank to a better position the colonel stopped him. He was, so it seemed, trying to make every possible mistake in the shortest possible time. I do not think he was a fifth columnist, but he couldn't have done much better for the enemy if he had been.

But as a final compromise, the colonel ordered the two other armored cars to stay on the south side as a reserve, and decided to send only two of our tanks across to the north side of the river. But all four of our antitank guns had to be on the north bank. The two 47-mm. antitank guns were placed some distance ahead of the northern ends of the two bridges to fire down the two main streets in Rouen. The two 25-mm. antitank guns were placed near the bridges in the street along the north bank of the Seine, one by the east bridge (Pont Cormeille) covering the approach to the bridge from the east, and one in front of the west bridge (Pont de Pierre) covering the approach to the bridge from the west. The motorized infantry was also to be kept on the north side, and likewise the motorcycle detachment. I was able to get the sidecars of this

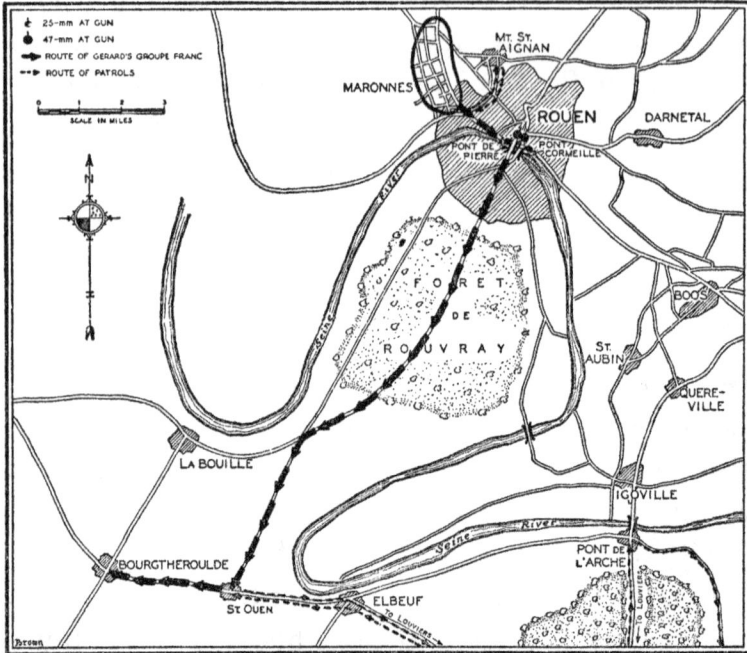

Map 4

detachment across to the south side, but the colonel abso-
lutely refused to let me get the infantry trucks and the antitank-gun prime-movers across to the French side of the
stream.

There was no time to dig in. We knew the Germans were
approaching for the colonel had received information that
the infantry unit sent to Boos to relieve us had been overrun
by a German mechanized column. But the antitank-gun crews
found enough sandbags to pile them up all around their guns.
These sandbags were white, however, and so did a good job
of advertising where the antitank guns were. It was necessary, to get any field of fire, to place the antitank guns right
in the middle of the street. Thus, with their backs to the river,
the crews were in effect being sacrificed by the colonel. On
the south side their chances of being killed would have been
less and they could have done a much more efficient job.

By now it was about 8:00 in the morning. A German observation plane circled around us, very slowly. We did not understand why the *Luftwaffe* was not already bombing us. Indeed, our whole situation there on the north side of the Seine seemed precarious. The two bridges had been previously mined, and at both ends of the bridges sandbag barricades had been installed. On the Pont Cormeille only an opening was left in the barricade so that military traffic could pass. This opening could be quickly closed by moving an old Renault tank from the last war into the opening. But my captain and I were not at all certain that the French captain of engineers would wait for us before he blew up the bridges.

And so in view of all this we looked at the Seine together and wondered whether we could get back across it after the bridges were blown. The river seemed mighty wide, and we were not so sure we could make it by swimming without getting hit by German bullets. After a thorough search along our bank by a few of our infantrymen, they found an abandoned rowboat. It was rather plump and heavy. But it was nevertheless a rowboat. I put one of our Foreign Legion men on guard over the boat. I had picked this particular man, a tough Yugoslav, for one sound reason: I knew he did not know how to row!

About that time I was summoned by my captain in a hurry. He said that one of the tank commanders was pretty nervous, that he had been shaken up badly in the battle of the day before. It would be better if I took that tank and fought with it. I had been trained to use the Somua tank at the Saumur Cavalry School and had participated in several problems and maneuvers. But now it was the real thing.

I figured my tank was to be sacrificed to fight on the north bank of the Seine. There was small hope of getting it back across after engaging the enemy. I checked my tank over and had all guns loaded, ready to fire. Then I found the commander of the other tank who was also the commander of the tank platoon. We decided that he with his tank would swing around to the rear of any German column that came down the streets of Rouen toward us, while I would attract the attention of the column from the front.

Suddenly, about 9:00, I heard a terrific noise. One of the antitank-gun crews had opened up, and we could also hear the shells from the German tanks in return. At once I headed my tank in the direction of the noise from a point near the banks of the Seine. As I did, the enemy's 88-mm. artillery which was apparently close behind their tanks began shelling the south bank of the Seine. The Germans undoubtedly thought we had established our defense on that bank. (They thought we were intelligent.) This was one time where doing the wrong thing helped, at least for a while.

I took my crew through side streets and was crossing the main road to the east bridge when I saw two German tanks coming down that long, straight street. I turned left toward them and stopped dead to fire with my 47-mm. gun at the leading tank. The French antitank-gun crew, farther away toward the bridge, ceased firing when they saw me heading toward the enemy. I missed my first shot, then zigzagged and advanced down the wide street, and then stopped and shot a second time. This time I got a direct hit on the turret of the German tank, but it still kept coming. I fired again and got a second hit, this time much lower, which disabled it. I was doing the firing myself, and my gunner was loading the 47-mm. gun as fast as he could.

Meanwhile, the other German tank was firing at me, but missed me twice; this one was still about 600 yards away. Advancing and zigzagging again, I made the mistake of firing a third shell at the tank I had already disabled. But I wanted to be sure to put the tank completely out of action.

Then I turned my turret toward the second German tank. The turret on the French Somua is power-driven and turns easily. As it turned I heard the definite whiz of an antitank shell passing close. I fired and missed the second German tank. And just as the gunner was loading my gun, my tank was terribly shaken by a hit—a hit with a 77-mm. shell from the German tank, which passed several inches below my feet and got, I think, my transmission. Nobody was wounded.

The driver tried the shifts forward. First gear did not work, second gear did not work; nor did any of the five forward speeds! There we were, apparently stuck and helpless, while the German had stopped firing, probably thinking he had killed the crew inside.

There was no hope of getting out of the tank, even through the escape trap, without being killed by the bullets of the enemy's machine guns. But then my driver thought of trying to back the tank, and the reverse gear worked, though with an awful noise. The tank moved slowly backwards, and painfully. But now the German tank, seeing that we moved again, resumed its fire at us. He wasn't much of a gunner, for he missed us again. The side of the street out of which we had come into the main street was too far back for us to have any hope of reaching before being hit by the German gun. There was only one thing to do—back the tank into a building.

I fired again at the German tank and missed it. I was just as poor a gunner as he was. Then we crashed backwards through a shop window and found ourselves in the middle of a grocery store, surrounded by empty shelves. Now we were sheltered from the antitank gun and machine guns of the German tank. But as we crawled out of our disabled tank, we could hear the enemy roaring down the street toward us.

Our position was rapidly becoming dangerous again. But luckily the brave antitank-gun crew guarding the bridge approach picked up its fire again, and apparently it destroyed

the German tank for the noise of its approach suddenly
stopped.

Just the same, there was no time to lose; we had to get
out of there. But first I had to blow up my tank. I did not
want the enemy to get a single piece of our equipment, even
just badly damaged. I always carried for this purpose in my
right-hand pocket two small *petards de cavalerie*, small
sticks of dynamite. And in my left pocket I had the two fuzes.
These had to be set very carefully, without too much friction;
otherwise the whole thing would explode. We put one stick
of dynamite in the chamber of our 47-mm. gun, and another
inside the tank, on the floor. Then we lighted the two fuzes and
headed fast for the back garden of the grocery shop. Exactly
ninety seconds later we heard the detonation: our tank was
blown up.

At the back of the garden we had to climb over a wall,
then over another into another back yard. We crossed this
yard, forced the door of a house, and walked through it. We
found ourselves in a small side street with no enemy in sight.

We ran full speed toward the river and there I found my
captain and reported what had happened. He bawled me out
in most severe terms for doing a poor job. He was right. My
tank had been destroyed and I had only put one German tank
out of commission. This was a big blow to our Groupe Franc.
For now we had only three tanks left.

By now more and more German tanks were coming toward our defensive area and shelling the antitank-gun positions as they came. All the while German artillery, on the hills
surrounding the city, kept pounding on the south side of the
Seine behind us. From what I saw and from the information
I gathered later from the different platoons of the Groupe
Franc, the enemy had about ten light tanks of the PzKw II
type (10 tons, crew of 3, 15-mm. armor, armament one 20-
mm. antitank gun and one light machine gun, maximum

speed 28 miles), and nearly 50 medium tanks of the PzKw IV type (weight 22 tons, crew of 5, 43-mm. armor, armament one 77-mm. antitank gun and two light machine guns, maximum speed 25 miles per hour). It was one of those PzKw IV's that put my tank out of commission.

In a city, tanks are naturally canalized by the buildings and easier to destroy. In order to limit to the minimum their chances of being hit, the German tanks adopted very interesting tactics. As I have said, the approaches to the bridges and our defenses ran north and south. The enemy tanks kept mainly on streets running east-west, and simply stopped for one or two seconds to fire every time they crossed the main street under fire of our antitank gun. Each time, they would fire one shell at the antitank gun defending a bridge, and then move full speed to the other bridge-approach street, and do the same thing against the antitank gun defending that bridge. Then they would go on across that street and turn south in a small street, thus gaining a street one block nearer to us, and then repeat the same procedure in the other direction. This gave our French antitank-gun crews only a brief glimpse of several German tanks crossing the main bridge-approach streets from east or west and at different ranges. It was no great wonder that our gun crews could not take care of them all; there were too many.

A few men at a time, the men of the antitank-gun crews were killed or wounded. New men came crawling toward the guns to take the place of their comrades and the guns kept steadily firing. In the course of the whole hard fight those two antitank guns destroyed fifteen German tanks for certain, and probably more. But the enemy was willing to take his losses, and kept on crossing the two main streets with his tanks and getting closer and closer every time.

Every time the German tanks crossed the two main streets, they would fire not only high-explosive shells, but also their

machine guns to keep new men from relieving the antitank-
gun crews and also to prevent the crews from retreating over
the bridges. Several of our infantrymen were killed bringing
ammunition to their comrades of the antitank guns. Here was
a splendid example of cooperation and sacrifice for the men
of another branch of the service—a thing that is only possible in a well-integrated combat team but utterly necessary
in modern war. Other infantrymen had installed their machine
guns in buildings along the main streets and kept firing at
the German tanks with armor-piercing bullets, but with little
effect.

Finally, as the situation grew tight, my captain ordered me
to cross the bridge and organize the defense of the south of
the Seine with what was left of the Groupe Franc. He decided
to keep the rowboat for himself and the last men over. As
long as the bridges were standing there was little point in
using the boat except that the bridges were under machine-
gun fire at frequent intervals. I wondered just how I would
be able to cross it with such machine-gun fire upon it. But it
had to be done. I went into one of the buildings near the
bridge to see the infantry platoon commander. He refused to
cross the bridge with me, saying he would cross later. He had
had a glimpse of a few German motorcycles in the distance
and wanted first to have a crack at them when they got closer.
I couldn't find our own platoon; they were somewhere in
some other buildings.

I came back to my captain and reported that the infantrymen wanted to stay. He looked pleased to know that his men
had such guts, but ordered me to cross the bridge just the
same and draw a sketch of the other side, indicating how we
could defend it to best advantage. The infantrymen would
follow me in a few minutes, he said. I never saw the infantry-
platoon commander again.

With the two other men of my tank crew and five or six others of the Groupe Franc, I crawled toward the bridge. By now the whole city was an inferno. The big oil tanks along the south side of the river in the western part of the city were being blown up and set afire by the French and from there we could hear tremendous explosions. Flames from the oil tanks leapt high in the air and gave off masses of black smoke. The noise of firing was terrific all around. Oil was flowing into the Seine. If the bridges were blown out now, how would our troops be able to swim in that gluey mess?

We kept crawling slowly ahead. We passed close to the antitank gun and I had a swift glimpse of the pile of wounded and dead around it. At that moment a German tank crossed the main street from right to left, stopped to fire down the middle of the street, but was behind another enemy tank that had been disabled by our antitank gun. This blown-up tank made fine cover for the German tank now firing.

A shell from the tank burst very close and slightly wounded the man behind me in the arm, but he decided to keep on across the bridge with me just the same. The German artillery, probably realizing by now that our defense was on the north side of the Seine, and not on the south side, began shortening its range. A few shells fell into the Seine itself, and then a few on the north bank behind me. These hit very near the place where I knew my captain was. Our Groupe Franc was getting a heavier dose than ever.

Now we started across the bridge, the men following me. We had some slight cover from the few sandbags at the north end of the bridge now behind us. We crawled, very slowly, and as flat as we could. Every time a German tank crossed the main street back there beyond the bridge, the bullets from its machine guns whistled only a few inches above us. At the Saumur Cavalry School my instructor had always had a terrible time to make us really crawl. I was doing it now to perfection.

Just as we reached the middle of the bridge I heard a great explosion and in amazement saw the east bridge go up in the air. The colonel in charge of our sector had blown up the bridge without any warning—without even removing the two armored cars stationed upon it. He had, so to speak, killed my friends. My instinctive reaction was that he might well give the same order for the bridge we ourselves were on. And so I decided to reach the south end of the bridge at full speed. Forgetting the machine-gun bullets, I stood up and ran as fast as I could. I signalled my men to follow, but they did not, and shouted that I should stay down, that I would get killed. Machine-gun bullets began to whistle again close by my ears. I literally threw myself on the bridge and began to pull myself on my stomach so that I could begin another rush from a different point. I had learned to do that again and again at the school and had hated the hard, gruelling practice. But I was doing it to save my life. As soon as the enemy machine guns stopped I stood up and ran again, this time a little longer, until again I could hear the bullets coming near me. And at last, in this manner, I reached a pillar of the bridge at the south side of the Seine.

At that moment came a tremendous blast and I felt myself hurled into the air. I landed on hands and face about twenty feet away, I still didn't know what had actually happened, when a great block of stone crashed on the ground a yard from my head. It was a part of the bridge I had just crossed on. I put my arms around my face and stayed flat and motionless. Other parts of the bridge were coming down but they were smaller chunks and had gone higher in the air. None of them hit me, but they came plenty close enough. Finally thousands of tiny fragments of the bridge came down upon me, making toc-toc-toc noises on my steel helmet. I wasn't hurt, only a few bruises. I looked behind me. The bridge was gone and so were my men. The antitank guns on the other side were silent now, probably destroyed. The good colonel had blown everything up nicely.

But the enemy tanks kept firing from across the river. I made a dash toward the first side street to reach cover from the fire. I found the south bank completely deserted. I decided to go to the public park south of the city where our trucks had been camouflaged. About then a few Stukas came over flying low and heading toward the south. Then I heard explosions at some distance. Could those planes be bombing our trucks, I tore toward the park, only a bit lame from what I had been through.

When I got there I found two trucks in flames. One was the telephone truck, the other the artillery heavy ammunition truck, and it was now a dangerous thing. Shell after shell from it kept exploding, then a case of small-caliber cartridges like a string of firecrackers. The drivers had already had a chance to move the other trucks far enough away to avoid any danger and were all admiring the free show! The other trucks had not been hit because they were under the trees and well apart from each other. The men told me that this was the first bombing in that part of town for a long time.

We could not conceive that the enemy would know just where the trucks had been parked and hidden without information from some fifth columnist. They had been well camouflaged, under big trees with thick foliage, and could hardly be seen from the air.

I left a few men to guard the vehicles and took all the other drivers, radiomen, telephone men, mechanics, and cooks, about thirty in all, packed them in sidecars of the motorcycle detachment, and headed back toward the Seine. Each man had a rifle, and we could at least prevent the enemy for a while from crossing the Seine on small rubber boats.

When we reached the Seine again to my surprise and pleasure I found my captain there with the commander of the

motorcycle detachment and his motorcyclists. They had just
crossed the river in the rowboat bringing the detachment over
in two trips. One of the motorcyclists was now rowing back
from the German side on the third trip and had several infantrymen in the boat. A few enemy motorcyclists arrived just
then along the shore and opened on the rowboat with their
light machine guns. Some of the men in the boat were killed,
others wounded, and the rest of our infantrymen were now
trapped in Rouen on the German side of the Seine. All four
antitank guns had been destroyed. But from the accounts of
the men from the motorcycle detachment, there were several
survivors of the antitank crews still over there on the north side.

The two armored cars we had left had not gone into action; they had been kept in reserve. We found them now in a
back street, waiting for orders from the colonel. But no sign
of the colonel. At that same time the two tanks we had in
reserve appeared. The commander of the tank the colonel had
put at the south end of the east bridge said that he had not
been able to fire a single shot, for fear of killing our own men,
who were in his line of fire on the enemy's tanks across the
river. He decidedly confirmed the fact that the two armored
cars on the bridge had not been warned, and were blown up
with the bridge. After the blowing up of the bridge, said this
tank commander, the colonel left for the south, apparently
badly shaken. The tank commander, with the bridge gone,
had been able to fire a few shots at German tanks. These tanks
then disappeared altogether from the main street and his field
of fire. When a few German motorcycles had appeared along
the north bank to the east, the tank commander fired at them,
probably wounding one or two. The others had left the bank
at once. Since then the tank commander had seen no more of
the enemy.

My captain came to a decision swiftly. It was a relief for
us to know that he was now in complete command and that

no elderly colonel, without knowledge of modern war, was superimposed over him any more. Two patrols of one armored car and a motorcycle squad each were now sent along the south shore of the Seine, one west and the other east. Our two tanks were kept behind as a mobile reserve. The mission of the small patrols was to observe along the banks of the Seine, fire at the enemy if they saw them, and keep them from crossing. The patrols were not to go more than five or six miles out from the city, and were to come back again to report. Meanwhile, the motorcycle detachment, dismounted, would stay near the destroyed bridges, observe, and fire with its six light machine guns at any Germans seen. We found a few sandbags around and used them to protect the machine-gun crews.

The German side of the Seine was now silent. Not an enemy man or tank in sight. But suddenly we heard firing—from a building on the south side, supposedly our own French side— somebody was firing at us from the rear. I had just time to run through a door into a near-by house to avoid the bullets. I then turned and shot at the windows of the building from which the fire was coming with my revolver. Two of our machine guns opened fire on the building too. Finally a motorcycle squad got into the building but found no one. But the fifth columnists had left a lot of small-arms ammunition in their haste.

By a stroke of luck, a little later on one of our men found an abandoned French 75-mm. gun in a small shack on the bank of the river. It had been so well camouflaged that none of us had seen it before. All around it plenty of shells were piled. My captain immediately decided to put the old gun to use. The emplacement for the gun nearby was excellent for we could fire pointblank at the other bank, and especially well at the point where the main street joined the river, right at the approach of the destroyed west bridge. My captain and I stayed near the gun, ready to fire. A few minutes later a tank appeared moving along the streets on the German side.

The motorcycle detachment held the fire of its machine guns. No use wasting ammunition against a tank. Then another tank appeared, going slowly and carefully, then a few motorcycles. We waited a minute more, then fired practically pointblank across the river at the tank and hit it. The range was only 400 yards and this first round set the tank on fire. Then our machine guns fired at the motorcycles.

The noise of a 75 is characteristic. When the Germans heard it they probably figured that a whole battery was facing them. They left the Seine as fast as they could move.

One of the houses on the German side began to burn, probably from our shelling. This building set the next afire, and soon the whole small area by the bridge approaches was in flames. I later read that the Germans had bombed this area. It would be more correct to say that my captain and I were responsible, not the bombs of the Germans.

Then my captain got a new idea. "Let's make a lot of noise, so the Germans will think that we're more powerful than we are, and maybe they won't try to cross for the rest of the day." By next day perhaps we could get some help from division headquarters, and hold on a little longer. Neither my captain nor I knew much about firing a 75, but we didn't do so badly. We simply guessed at elevations and deflections, and we could see the impact of our shells along the hills beyond the northern part of the city. German batteries fired back and shelled us accurately. It began to get uncomfortable but we kept on until our ammunition was practically exhausted. We knew that the enemy blitzkrieg tactics avoided the strongpoints in the enemy lines. We hoped to create the impression of a strongpoint where we were. Whether the Germans were fooled or not, they never once tried to cross the river Seine at Rouen.

Along about 1:00 in the afternoon, a motorcycle scout sent by division headquarters came with an order for us to retreat, and defend a new position from La Bouille on the Seine in the west to Elbeuf on the Seine in the east. Around Rouen the river makes a big loop and Rouen is exactly at the top of the loop, with La Bouille and Elbeuf on the two sides at the bottom of the loop. By establishing this line, our front would be greatly shortened. The division commander, however, had overlooked one fact. By abandoning Rouen, we left the Germans free to establish a bridgehead there, unmolested, and to pour all their armored equipment upon us from there. We would have much preferred to stay along the Seine, even though it meant some ten more miles of front. At least we would know what was going on, and whether or not the enemy was attempting a crossing.

So we left Rouen reluctantly, and established our own headquarters at St. Ouen, between Elbeuf and La Bouille. On the road to St. Ouen, we were bombed and machine-gunned by Stukas, and lost three sidecars.

At La Bouille, where the river was very narrow and the Germans might attempt a crossing, we found about fifty British. At Elbeuf we discovered many refugees and some French infantry units in full flight. A little north of St. Ouen, we came across what was left of an infantry battalion. The battalion commander, a rather young and energetic lieutenant colonel, had decided to stay and fight. Since there was no sign of the enemy and no indication that the enemy would attempt a crossing that afternoon, we decided to give the survivors of the Groupe Franc a well-earned rest.

I was practically exhausted myself but my captain called me and the commander of the motorcycle detachment for a small conference to talk over the means left at our disposal. In those few hours of fighting, our Groupe Franc had taken a terrific mauling. And the one main reason was we had fought on the north side of the Seine instead of defending from its south bank.

What we had left was just the ghost of what we had been. We still had two tanks and two armored cars, the motorcycle detachment with fifteen sidecars, plus three gasoline trucks, two ammunition trucks, and the kitchen, maintenance, radio and supply trucks. Out of approximately 220 men at the beginning of the Battle of Rouen, we had 90 left. But only half of these were combatant troops. Of our eight officers only three were left. The situation was not so good.

As soon as we finished sizing up the situation, my captain sent me by sidecar to Pont de l'Arche (see map 4), on the Seine, fifteen miles to the east, to see whether the other Groupe Franc was still around there. All we knew was that it had been in Igoville the night before. Igoville was just a few miles north of Pont de l'Arche, on the German side of the Seine. If the enemy had already crossed at Pont de l'Arche, I was to return as fast as I could. If I found the other Groupe Franc, I was to bring back all the information they had.

I started for Pont de l'Arche with my private driver, a motorcycle racer in civilian life. The only armament we had was my own revolver, and my driver's rifle. We crossed through Elbeuf like a streak, cutting our way through the refugees. But beyond Elbeuf we saw no one.

For the first time that day I really relaxed. The wind felt good and kept me awake. We were not on the road to Pont de l'Arche that follows the Seine, which was too exposed, but on a roughly parallel route farther back from the river. This route turned left toward Pont de l'Arche just before reaching Louviers. We passed through forest near Louviers, still alone. But soon, in an opening in the forest we came to a battery of 155-mm. guns. The battery had been left alone there with no protection. But apparently they were not worried. They were singing as they camouflaged their guns very carefully, and were preparing to fire at targets on the other side of the river.

By then the road was sloping gently toward the banks of the river. We could see the hills on the German side a few miles beyond the river. If the enemy is there, I thought, he has a perfect view of this road. I ordered my driver to go even faster.

We found the village completely deserted. No sign at all of the other Groupe Franc. I got out of my sidecar and crawled toward the Seine. The bridge was blown but no enemy in sight. The Germans could have crossed, at that time, unmolested. And why they did not I still do not know. Probably the advanced units of the German panzer division were too far ahead of their other troops.

Just then I heard noise of motors and rumblings of tracks behind me on my own side of the Seine. A German column? I hurried toward the central square of the village, where I had left my sidecar. From there I could see coming down the road I had followed myself a long French column of *dragons portés* (motorized troops) sent to take up a position near Pont de l'Arche, along the Seine. Then I suddenly heard the whistling of 88-mm. shells from across the Seine, and I could see that their targets were the first vehicles in the French column. The Germans could not have had a better target. They had an unobstructed view, the road was straight, and on both sides of it were thick woods, into which the half-tracks of the *dragons portés* could not expect to penetrate. The battalion commander had made the mistake of having his whole battalion advance on this dangerous stretch at the same time, instead of using small movements of a platoon.

What I saw then was the terribly destructive effect of an accurately placed artillery concentration on a motorized column, and how helpless such a column is under such fire. First the column tried to speed up to get down to the village where the vehicles could turn left or right into the streets for cover. But as truck after truck was hit, the road was finally blocked, and the rest of the column could not move at all.

The French battalion then abandoned the idea of saving their vehicles. Men dashed from the trucks to find cover in the woods. But the enemy's shelling grew heavier. Shells killed troops as they tried to get out of their vehicles. And the German artillery opened their fire to include the woods on each side of the road.

Then a shell burst near me down in the village, but did not injure me or my driver because we were flat on the ground. I was no longer a spectator now. We ran to the shell hole and kept down in it.

After about thirty minutes the shelling stopped for a short while but picked up again for ten or fifteen minutes more. But now the French artillery began to pound the German side and silenced the German battery.

I had left my motorcycle in a garage on the main square of the town. This was almost the only building around that square still standing. The back of the garage had been de-molished, but my motorcycle was OK. I decided to leave as fast as I could. But first I talked to a few of the officers of the motorized unit who were still alive and was happy to find there one of my instructors in antitank defense at Saumur. None of the officers had expected the Germans to be already on the other side of the Seine. I finally left Pont de l'Arche, taking a small dirt road back to the east. I didn't want the enemy to repeat his show just for my sidecar.

We were travelling along this road at good speed when we came upon a clearing, with only big trees a short distance apart along the sides of the road. At that moment I heard the droning of a plane coming close. I looked up and saw a lone German bomber heading toward us. For a German bomber to spend his time and ammunition in attacking a single side-car on a road seemed pure sadism, the pleasure of killing for killing. We ran off the road and took cover in the ditch along it. Evidently the enemy flyer was returning from a mission, and had used all his bombs, for he didn't drop any. He just machine-gunned us, circling and diving to get as good aim as possible. Now my driver and I hugged close to the trunk of sizable trees, he on one side of the road and I on the other. As the plane circled, so did we around our big trees. It seems funny now, but it was deadly serious then. And our careful timing in moving around and around like squirrels was the only thing that saved us.

Finally the enemy pilot gave up and soared away. Our motorcycle had one flat tire from a bullet, so we had to change it. The sidecar itself was riddled with bullets.

When we got back to our Groupe Franc headquarters, I thought I could relax for a while and sleep. But not this time either. The captain had received an order from division head-quarters to move us at full speed to Bourgtheroulde, a small town about six miles to the west. The captain directed me to prepare everything for the move.

But as we began to pull out from under the apple trees under which the vehicles had been camouflaged, seventeen enemy planes appeared. We hit the ditches. The Germans dropped about a dozen bombs, not from a dive, but from a straight low flight. One bomb fell near me in the middle of the road, but all its fragments passed over my head. I was only spattered thoroughly with mud. The bomb was a very small one; the hole it made was only about two feet deep in the road. It did, however, kill several refugees not far away.

We were almost untouched by this bombing, and as soon as it stopped went on to Bourgtheroulde, where we found part of the town in flames from an attack by the same enemy bombers. Remnants of the French Army and refugees kept pouring into the place, all going south. We had to work extremely hard to prevent a bad traffic jam from developing. The refugees and British and French troops were also looting stores. This didn't help our preparations for the defense of the village either. For these and other reasons we definitely didn't like the place.

III: Defense Behind the Seine

After all the movements our Groupe Franc had made, which I have told about in the earlier parts of this account, its gasoline was running dangerously low. My captain accordingly decided to send me with two gasoline trucks to get some more, wherever I could find it. We could no longer count on supplies coming up from the rear. We could only count on ourselves.

I left on June 10th at 3:00 in the morning, with two drivers and two other men to help. At one gas station after another we found the pumps empty. We tried all the gas stations from Bourgtheroulde to Pont Audemer and all those in Pont Audemer itself—but no gas. I then gave up as far as that particular area was concerned, and decided to drive straight south for thirty miles, without stopping, to reach Lisieux, a good-sized town with a big Standard Oil tank depot near it.

There was nobody at the depot except two or three workers and an old French janitor. I told him I wanted a thousand gallons of gasoline for our Groupe Franc, whereupon he asked me to give him a blue requisition slip, Form No. 3. I had none of course, and told him so, but "No slip, no gas," was all I could get out of him. I tried argument and even plead with him, telling him that if I didn't get the gas he alone would be responsible for the death and capture of the men of our

Groupe Franc, who were, after all, defending him. But he could not rise from his long life of routine and Forms No. 3 to conceive a different world.

I finally cut things short, pulled my revolver out and said I would shoot him if he didn't give us the gas. He just about collapsed, but had strength enough left to call me a gangster. But we got the gas. And not just a thousand gallons, but 1,500 gallons more in big barrels, more even than my two trucks could quite carry. I had also learned one fast way to cut red tape.

We then headed back toward the north and the front. On the runningboard of each truck I kept a man standing and constantly watching the sky for planes. It seemed a good idea not to be caught without warning while we were still in the gasoline trucks.

In a short time we were driving against the flow of refugees, and as we passed through Brionne there were houses still burning from a bombardment a short while before. As we came to Bourgtheroulde, however, the refugees and fleeing troops grew fewer and fewer. "The Germans are already in Bourgtheroulde," some of them cried. But they all seemed in a state of semi-hysteria, and in such a state false rumors spread at terrific speed. We did advance very slowly toward Bourgtheroulde, but found no enemy. Our Groupe Franc was still there. And the men acclaimed the arrival of more gas as if it had been gold. In short order it was distributed to the vehicles.

The captain then decided to move his headquarters platoon to a small hamlet off the main road, two miles to the southwest of Bourgtheroulde, where the vehicles would be more secure. That morning he had sent two patrols, each consisting of an armored car and a few motorcycles, to La Bouille and to Elbeuf. But not a single German had they seen. The enemy was still not attempting to cross the Seine.

In the afternoon of that day (June 10th) my captain received information from division headquarters that supposedly sixty German parachutists had just landed to the south of the Seine, in the loop below Rouen, and had sought cover in the woods of the Forêt de Rouvray. The captain decided to send me there to find out what the situation actually was. There were only a few sidecar motorcycles left. So I got only one for the job. But my driver and I were equipped. Each of us had a light machine gun and two revolvers, and several hand grenades besides. And as my captain put it, before we left, if I didn't get back within three hours he would know that there were parachutists in the Forêt de Rouvray.

We followed a small dirt road, winding through the woods. Our motorcycle noisily advertised our approach, and if there were any parachutists posted along the road it was not going to be hard for them to kill us. I rode with both feet hanging outside the "bathtub," ready to hit the ditch along the road. As we approached every curve, we stopped to observe and listen intently. But not a sound. And not a German. We kept on toward Rouen and reached the suburbs. And then we took a small street leading to the Seine. The whole city was deserted. At the river we dismounted and watched the far bank where the two bridges, now demolished, had led. As we did this we held our light machine guns in our arms like two movie gangsters. But still we saw no German soldier. After a little we jumped in our sidecar and headed back full speed on the straight main road. What headquarters had told us was just another false rumor.

Not far out of St. Ouen and Bourgtheroulde, we were suddenly stopped by a group of French infantrymen hidden along the road. They sprang out at us with light machine guns and rifles at the ready. The sergeant in charge announced that I was under arrest and they all surrounded us, looking as if they meant serious business. I told them that I was a French

officer from the Groupe Franc, coming back from a reconnaissance, but they did not believe me. I showed my officer's
card with my fingerprints and photograph, but they were still
suspicious. They took us to the young infantry lieutenant in
command of their platoon. He too was fully as suspicious. In
the end we were dragged to the lieutenant colonel commanding the infantry battalion, who recognized me, as I had met
him the day before. Apparently these troops, misled by our
special equipment and particularly by the new armored-force
helmets we were wearing, padded in front with leather, had
mistaken us for German parachutists. Back in Bourgtheroulde
I reported the negative results of my patrol.

To my great astonishment I found there the commander
of the tank platoon whom I thought had been killed in Rouen.
He was the one who had gone out with his tank to hit the
rear of the German column, north of Rouen. His attack had
been a successful surprise. He had destroyed three German
tanks, then retreated full speed. A little later he had attacked
the flank of the tank column that was in the city itself and
got two more enemy tanks, about the time we had been fighting those same tanks hardest with our antitank guns. His tank
was hit once, in the left of the cupola, but this did not disable
it. He could still fire the gun, however, and managed to get
hits on two more German tanks.

Then he had heard the two explosions of the bridges and
decided he might be able to get back across the Seine with
his tank on one of the ferries. The ferry at La Bouille had
been destroyed, so he went as far as Caudebec and was
amazed not to encounter a single enemy column all the way.
At Caudebec he found the ferry still operating but had a hard
time putting his tank on it, though he finally got it aboard.
In the middle of the Seine the ferry was machine-gunned by
a lone bomber but three RAF pursuit planes which suddenly
appeared opened on the German plane and drove it away.

Landed safely on the south side of the Seine, the tank-platoon commander had to spend all the next day (June 9th) hunting for some gasoline. He kept asking all fleeing troops and refugees whether they had seen a French motorized unit with our Groupe Franc numeral painted in white on the sides of the vehicles, and was finally directed to Bourgtheroulde. He had some trouble, he reported, dodging colonels who wanted to commandeer his tank to ride in as they retreated to the south.

I had just about time to hear this story when some German bombers came in sight. Not far away from where I was there was an old 75-mm. gun in position, guarding one of the roads to the town. The officer in charge of it had lost his unit in the general retreat and had offered his services to my captain, who had gladly accepted. The German planes had first dropped a few bombs on the central square of the town near the church. Suddenly, as they came directly overhead, a man left a small group of refugees not far away and ran toward the 75-mm. gun, waving a white cloth. One of the planes saw it, diving straight on the gun which was well-camouflaged, and had apparently not been seen from the air before. The plane released three bombs, one after the other, and got the small crew of the 75 and the officer. But it also killed the fifth columnist, too, in the middle of his dirty work. The gun was no longer usable.

That same night we heard a sudden shot in the street of the village. On investigation we found one of our men lying dead, with his papers gone and the identification plate on his wrist likewise stolen. By now this continual fifth column activity had gotten thoroughly on our nerves. We began to hate such activities more than anything else, except attacks from the air.

The next morning, June 11th, came one of the best surprises of the whole campaign. On a stolen bicycle, dirty,

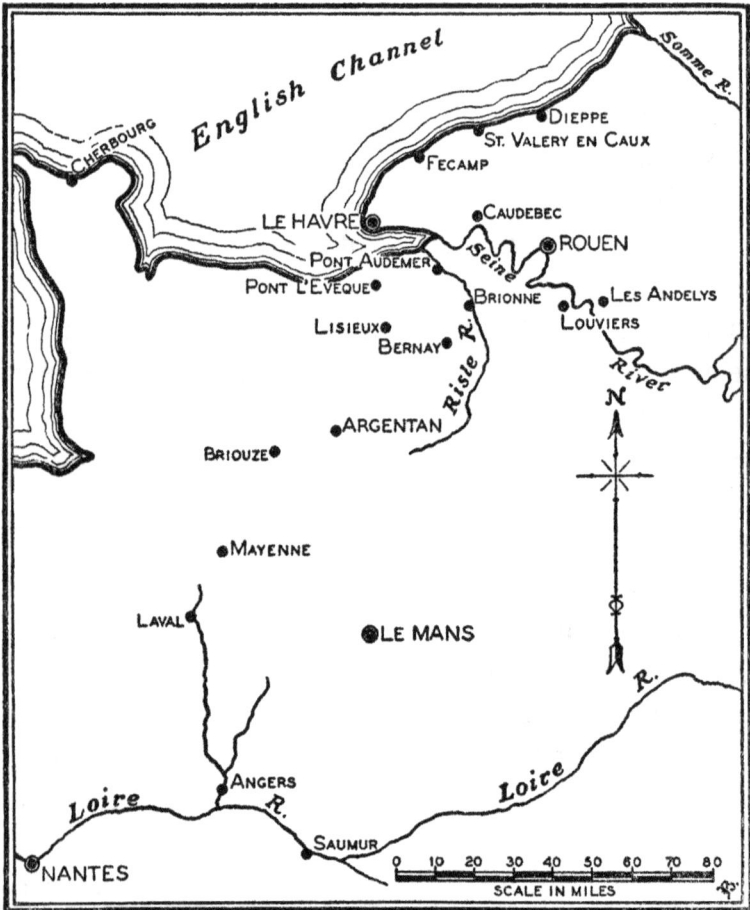

Map 5: General map Rouen-Le Mans-Nantes

unshaved, and exhausted, came riding into Bourgtheroulde the first lieutenant who commanded our 25-mm. antitank-gun platoon, and whom we had also thought had been killed in the battle of Rouen two days before. He told us, moreover, that ten miles from Bourgtheroulde there were thirty infantry-men whom he had brought back from the north side of Rouen, and also the remnants of our antitank-gun crews—a few like himself who had survived the blowing of the bridges and the German artillery fire. At once we gave him two trucks to bring these men back to us.

When he returned, two hours later, the lieutenant explained that the blowing of the bridge had put his antitank guns out of commission and killed nearly everyone in their crews. Those still alive had luckily found the men of the infantry platoon. Together they all marched toward the west along the banks of the Seine. A few miles out from Rouen they found a barge that would float. On this they got across to the south side, fifteen miles from Rouen, between Duclair and Caudebec. They marched from there toward Pont Audemer, inquiring as they went about our Groupe Franc. But soon they were so exhausted that the lieutenant ordered them to rest, and continued the search himself with a commandeered bi-cycle, in the end finding us in Bourgtheroulde.

Almost unbelievably our Groupe Franc was now regain-ing some of its past strength. We were now five officers and about 120 men. The infantrymen had brought back four of their six heavy machine guns and this boosted our fire power a little. On the other hand, we had a new and serious prob-lem because these thirty additional men had lost all their trucks—all transportation of every kind—and we could only cram them in the few vehicles we had left. But this, compared to the joy of getting them back, was a small thing.

What we were concerned about more deeply was our ammu-nition. It was low, after our battles at Boos and Rouen. But I got word from some retreating British that there was an abandoned munitions train on one of the railroad tracks near La Bouille in the middle of the forest. Immediately I took one of our trucks and four men to the spot, where we found the train. Near its front part and its rear part were enormous bomb craters, but by some miracle the attacking Nazis planes had missed the part that carried the ammunition. I posted a man in front of the train and another in its rear to give the rest of us warning with their whistles if any plane approached.

The bomb craters, the half-demolished train, the dead silence of the place, the lack of human activity, gave us the feeling that we were far from substantial military protection, and exposed to any sudden attack. Nervously we opened door after door of the freight cars. This took time, for the doors were all sealed. We looked rapidly inside each car to see whether it had the boxes of ammunition in it. All the first cars we opened contained artillery shells for 155-mm. and 75-mm. guns.

Suddenly one of the men whistled three times. We dashed across the tracks and under the train into the woods on the other side, as three planes came over. They let go a few bombs in level flight, but missed the ammunition train. We let our breaths out, crawled back again to the train, and in a few minutes more found what we wanted. We jammed one truck full as fast as we could, took the load back to the Groupe Franc, and then made a second trip to load the second ammunition truck. During the time we had three alerts, and had to hit cover three times, but no bombs were dropped on us.

When we came back from the wrecked ammunition train the second time the Groupe Franc was about ready to leave Bourgtheroulde for a small village some fifteen miles to the west called Bourneville. During the movement I performed the job of *serrefile,* that of the officer who is last in the column and sees to it that no vehicle is lost and that those with motor troubles get repaired and catch up. But no vehicle had such trouble this time. The mechanics had spent all night overhauling their motors and checking all possible weaknesses. Several Nazi planes machine-gunned us on the way to Bourneville, but their aim was bad and we had no casualties.

According to the reports of our patrols, there were still no signs that the enemy had tried a crossing anywhere in our sector. We had sent patrol after patrol along the Seine all day, in rotation, of course, to enable our men to get some rest. We now had to rely on continuous reconnaissance of this type because we had lost our radio truck in the bombardment of Bourgtheroulde, which had been a major blow for the Groupe Franc. Without a radio truck, we were continually losing contact with our armored cars and tanks during their march, and we were cut off from information from higher headquarters except for the news brought by the few motorcycle scouts that we could spare and keep stationed all the time with corps headquarters to bring us orders and new information on the latest developments.

Late in the evening of June 11th we arrived at Bourneville, a charming little village still full of refugees. It had not been bombed. We immediately felt better because of this peaceful atmosphere, even though the degree of danger here was exactly the same as it had been at Bourgtheroulde. We were lucky to find there also a few lambs and sheep, which we killed and ate with much delight. No food, of course, was reaching us from the rear, and we were getting sick of eating our *pain de guerre*, a very dry hardtack, and the cans of *singe* ("monkey meat" or canned beef) which we had in our supply truck. It was even luckier to find 400 pounds of flour in the town bakery, and we immediately detailed two men to make some bread. For the next two days these men made bread without taking a single minute of rest. It tasted better than any bread I ever ate in my life.

We camouflaged our trucks in two orchards as soon as we arrived in the village. Beginning at once, also, and all during the night, the men constructed roadblocks on all roads at the outskirts of the village. We took over the central switchboard at the post office simply by telling the girl in charge that the Germans were approaching full speed—another way of cutting red tape. She left at once, scared to death. Once an hour during the night we sent a patrol, on foot, around the village, mainly to listen. In the village the patrol saw to it that there were no lights, not even a match or a cigarette.

The next morning, June 12th, my captain and I went around the village to determine the best emplacements for the heavy machine guns of the motorized infantry platoon. We were walking along a little, dirt road just outside of the village when suddenly, not fifty yards away, a man appeared and aimed a submachine gun directly at us. We threw ourselves into the ditch along the road as bullets whistled past our ears, automatically pulling our revolvers as we did so. My captain killed the German with his second shot. When we examined the fifth columnist and his little gun we found that he had fired some sixty bullets at us. This Mauser submachine gun of the Germans is a very inaccurate weapon though its use had a marked psychological effect on the population. We found no identification papers on the German, only a map of the region. It was more detailed than the official French military maps we were using.

Since German fifth columnists were apparently mingled in with French refugees, my captain decided to take stern measures. We prepared a lot of small notices and pasted these on the walls of the village. The notice declared that to avoid any possibility of fifth columnist activity and enable us to prepare our defense without being hampered by refugees, the commander of the Groupe felt compelled to order every civilian to leave the village within an hour. After two hours had passed any civilian found in the village without good reason would be locked up and, if there seemed grounds for it, shot. During the rest of the campaign we executed several. We may have made a mistake or two but most of them were in all probability fifth columnists and all others had been warned. Until we took this stern action, no matter how well our vehicles had been camouflaged, German bomber pilots always seemed to know where they were hidden. But from then on, we suffered very few bombings in any village we defended. I feel therefore that the drastic measures taken by my captain were justified.

Bourneville was to be the headquarters of our Groupe Franc. We were not only assigned this village to defend, but also were assigned a line to protect behind the Seine that had a front of about twenty-five miles—from La Bouille near Rouen to the sea. To hold any such front with 120 men was practically an impossible task. If the enemy tried to cross by force it was evident we could not prevent them from doing so. We could, however, hinder their preparations on the far bank and could probably repulse any crossing attempted by a weak reconnaissance force. Our main mission, however, was that of warning the division headquarters of any crossing attempt. Thus we were, in effect, the rear guard of the French division. What puzzled me during that time was the fact that none of us had ever seen this division. Was it a myth, a ghost, or just a bunch of men too afraid to fight in the front lines? Or was it just retreating slowly on foot to new positions? I found out on June 18th, a few days later, when I actually saw the men in the division surrounded.

A company of customs officers on bicycles retreating from the coast came into our area. They wore vivid blue uniforms with a red stripe down their pants. Their commander had very little push and my captain persuaded him to stay with us, telling him he would have nothing to do, that my captain would take care of everything. We naturally welcomed any reinforcements as long as they would stay with us.

We set up our defense in the following manner. All along the banks of the river we posted these 300 customs officers with their rifles. (They had no machine guns.) Thus they were used as a line of sentries or scouts about 150 yards apart. Every two or three miles a sidecar or a solo motorcycle from the Groupe Franc was posted. If one of the customs officers saw the enemy trying to cross the Seine, or preparing to make such a crossing, he was to fire several shots with his rifle to attract the attention of the motorcyclist, who would at once go to the place where the shots came from and then report to the headquarters of the Groupe Franc on the situation. At certain places the motorcyclist could use a telephone nearby instead of racing to headquarters.

We installed the headquarters of our Groupe Franc in the post office of Bourneville. As map 6 shows, the town lay several miles south of the Seine behind a deep forest and we made it the strongpoint of our defense, preparing its immediate defenses with mechanized attack mainly in mind. For the fixed defenses of the village the captain used the motorized infantry platoon, the several roadblocks, and a 47-mm, antitank-gun platoon under the energetic young artillery officer who had lost his unit and offered his services and those of his platoon to my captain instead of fleeing to the south like most of the rest of the army. His two antitank guns with their prime-movers and the one cargo truck with them were a great help to us and made up for our losses in the fight at Rouen.

The most essential part of our defense was the mobile reserve formed of two armored cars, the motorcycle platoon, and our three remaining tanks. The armored cars and motorcyclists were used also to effect numerous reconnaissances to the east, in order to cover our right flank if the Germans

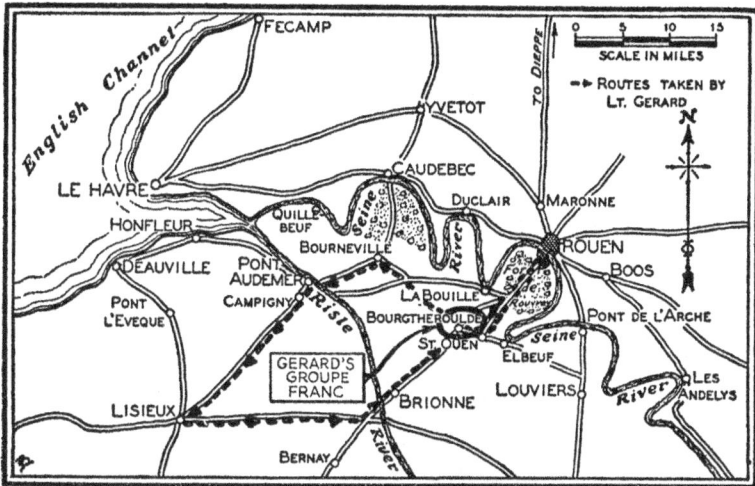

Map 6: Defense along the Seine

crossed the Seine east of Rouen. Our three tanks were ordered to go back and forth along the south bank of the Seine. Once an hour one of the tanks left La Bouille in the direction of Quillebeuf, moving along the Seine, stopping often to observe the other bank, and firing at any Germans who were sighted. The tank would come back to La Bouille again after a few hours. Thus our three tanks were constantly scouting along the Seine at different points, toward different directions. We hoped by using them that way to give the enemy the impression that there was a sizable mechanized force on the south side of the Seine, and thus make them hesitate to attempt a crossing. I doubt very much whether we actually fooled the Germans, but at least if they attempted a crossing, our fire would certainly harass them and slow them up. If the enemy tried to cross anywhere our three tanks were to assemble full speed and concentrate their fire on the point the customs officer sentries indicated.

I did a good deal of that back-and-fourth business in a tank myself because the tank platoon commander was worn out and needed a rest. On the first day I saw nothing of the enemy, driving all the time with my turret open. Nor did our patrols to the east report any Germans either. When night came we drove our three tanks back to Bourneville, and that first night I stayed near the telephone with my captain.

About 2:00 o'clock in the morning (June 13th) the telephone rang and one of the motorcyclists told us that between Duclair and Caudebec a German motorized infantry column was moving along the north bank of the Seine on the road that followed the river. Some of the customs officers had fired across at them to give the alarm, and at once the enemy had returned the fire, using tracer bullets of all possible colors— red, white, blue, yellow. The effect on the customs officers of seeing that kind of a show was terrific; they had never seen such a thing. Half an hour later another motorcyclist phoned. The German column, he said, was still advancing to the west along the river bank and was now keeping up a terrific noise for the purpose, he thought, of scaring our defending troops. The enemy would send a red rocket into the sky, and the whole column would stop dead. Then a green rocket would go up and the column would resume its march. They also used white and yellow rockets for some purpose, and the whole performance was more than puzzling. From our own side of the Seine our motorcyclists and customs officers could hear officers shouting orders in German, and even the enemy troops singing Nazi songs. The few customs officers who took up fire with their rifles didn't seem to bother the column, which was returning their fire with tracer bullets, now from machine guns. But daylight approached without any attempt by the enemy to cross the river.

At 5:00 o'clock that morning I again left Bourneville with my tank and resumed scouting along the Seine, but with much more care than before because we knew for sure now that enemy troops were on the other side. Beyond Duclair I saw a few Germans but no vehicles. I systematically shelled their general area with the high-explosive shells of my 47-mm. gun and must have killed a few. I opened fire from a defiladed position with good protection against antitank-gun fire. But apparently the German force had no antitank guns with it and only returned the fire with small automatic arms. That kind of fighting continued at intermittent periods all during the day.

I learned later why the Germans had not appeared on the north side of the Seine right after our battle in Rouen. Contrary to our belief the panzer division whose reconnaissance units we had met in Boos and Rouen, did not stay along the Seine but headed northwest toward the sea and reached the sea at St. Valery-en-Caux, a little southwest of Dieppe, thus completely encircling the French and British troops retreating from the Somme River. Only when they had partly cleared up this pocket did the German motorized infantry turn south to take position along the lower part of the Seine between Rouen and the sea.

During the afternoon of June 13th, as I arrived opposite Caudebec, I saw that the whole town was in flames. The Germans had just bombed the place. And all along the road leading to the ferry were hundreds of abandoned automobiles, all on fire with flames leaping into the sky. On my way back to Bourneville, early that evening, I met a few British who had built a beautiful roadblock on the road my tank was following in the middle of the forest. They had two antitank rifles to defend it, but were preparing to leave which they soon did. They left a lot of equipment behind, which we salvaged eagerly the next day—excellent motorcyclists' goggles, some good light raincoats, and especially the two antitank rifles which they had evidently decided were too heavy for them to carry in their hasty retreat. We liked that particular antitank weapon, of which our army had none. It was called the Boys rifle from its inventor and was of caliber .55, weighing around thirty-six pounds with its bipod rest. It was effective against lightly armored vehicles at short distances.

I spent the night again at the telephone with my captain. One rumor after another to the effect that the Germans had crossed the Seine east of Rouen came to us over the phone. Louviers, a bridgehead on our side of the Seine, south of Pont de l'Arche, was reported in German hands. The German column was advancing at night, toward the east, toward us, we were also told. To determine the part of reality and the part of fantasy in those rumors was impossible, except by sending out our own patrols. At 2:00 in the morning a colonel telephoned us from division headquarters. He said a German column was already a few miles from Bourneville, in Bourgtheroulde, our last previous position. If this was true our position with our right flank exposed was now untenable. The colonel wanted a patrol sent at once to confirm this information. My captain told him that to send out a tank at night on such a mission was hardly desirable. The tank couldn't see anything anyway and could be taken in ambush. It was finally decided to send a tank and a few motorcycles with machine guns at dawn. My captain told me that I had been inside a tank enough during the past two days, and that I should therefore wake up the tank-platoon commander and direct him to take charge of the patrol. In view of the importance of this patrol my captain decided to send an entire motorcycle platoon with its commander.

This patrol left Bourneville at 4:30 on the morning of June 14th. We waited and waited, until an hour later one of the men of the motorcycle platoon reported by telephone. The patrol had been mistaken for a German column by the French artillery still in Bourgtheroulde which had opened fire. Several men were wounded, and the tank-platoon commander was dying. The motorcycle-platoon commander asked us to send a truck at once to transport the wounded to the nearest hospital or ambulance. My captain sent me with a truck and telephoned division headquarters to send two ambulances at once to Bourneville. Arriving in front of Bourgtheroulde, I saw the disabled tank near the road. In Bourgtheroulde itself, I found the motorcycle-platoon commander who told me the story very briefly.

The tank commander with his tank was out in front of the motorcycle platoon. He was fired at without warning from the outskirts of Bourgtheroulde. Thinking it was enemy fire, he quickly returned it. The motorcycle platoon dismounted and sought cover in the ditches along the road, opening on the supposed enemy with their machine guns. The "Germans" were firing with a 77-mm. or 75-mm. gun, well camouflaged. Its high-explosive shells burst near the motorcycle platoon. The tank kept on firing shells at the gun, using fire and movement, stopping only to fire. After a couple of minutes the tank received a direct hit on its front and the shell penetrated the tank as if through butter. Fragments of armor cut the left arm off the driver and tore the gunner's right shoulder apart. Another piece went through the tank-platoon commander's helmet into his head.

The motorcycle platoon advanced along the road in the ditches, approaching the village, to determine the strength of the enemy forces, but they finally discovered that the enemy was French. Our tank had killed two men of the artillery gun crew. The tank commander was in bad shape when I arrived with the truck and was plainly dying. I carried the wounded back to Bourneville as fast as I could, and from there they were taken to the rear in two ambulances.

The mistake had occurred partly because of the morning fog. The artillerymen couldn't determine whether the tank was French or German. Our tanks had the blue-white-and-red circle of the Republic, and German tanks had the Iron

Cross painted on the front of the tank. But the Germans had used French colors so many times that this means of identification was of little practical value. Since the French had so little mechanized equipment left in the area, the artillerymen could hardly be wrong in assuming that any mechanized equipment they would see would be German. The real reason for the mistake was because the crews of the artillery anti-tank guns had never had any thorough training in identifying the silhouettes of the different types of French, British, and German vehicles. And, of course, the lack of liaison between division headquarters and this particular artillery unit gave rise to the rumors that the Germans were there in Bourgtheroulde, and prevented the artillery unit from being warned in time that a French mechanized patrol was approaching.

The tank commander was also somewhat at fault. He would probably not have been killed if he had stayed with his tank along the edge of the woods west of Bourgtheroulde, and sent a few motorcycles to reconnoiter the village before he exposed his tank in the perfectly flat, open area between the woods and the village. With hindsight, however, it is always easy to criticize an action that has proved disastrous. Anyway, the result was a serious blow to the Groupe Franc. We now had only two armored cars and two tanks left as armored equipment. We had also lost a few sidecar motorcycles, destroyed by the 75-mm. fire in the same fight.

Shortly after I had come back to Bourneville, we received an order from headquarters to retreat again. Other rumors that the Germans had crossed the River Seine east of Rouen had been confirmed by other units. Our movement had to be effected quickly, otherwise a German column advancing generally toward the southwest would cut our retreat. Our Groupe Franc was ordered to go to Campigny and establish its headquarters in this little village a few miles southeast from Pont Audemer, and prepare a defense behind a small

river, the Risle. The French Army as a whole was abandoning the Seine as a defensive position.

What made us smile a bit at this news was that as far as
we had been able to see, the Seine had never been defended
by French forces at all, except for a few rear-guard units like
our own. All during the time we had been making reconnaissance after reconnaissance from one position after another
behind the Seine, our division had been stationed back there
behind the Risle, building a few roadblocks. And now that
the Seine line had been dented, our division was leaving the
Risle and we were to take their place there. Things went this
way, in fact, up to June 18th, when the division was surrounded. During the whole time it did not fire a single shot
to the best of our knowledge. For its own retreat, the division was lucky enough to have great numbers of Paris buses
which the Army had requisitioned. Without those buses it
would probably have been captured a few days sooner.

My captain used our two tanks to protect the rear of our
column as we dropped back from Bourneville to Campigny.
The two armored cars, with what was left of the motorcycle
platoon, protected our flanks by making small reconnaissances out on side roads, coming back to the main road after
the column had passed. Thus the column had a mobile antitank defense on its flanks and rear. No hasty roadblocks were
built on the side roads because this would take too much time
and work. Instead, my captain relied on the armored cars to
repulse any small German mechanized column during the
time it would take to reestablish the Groupe Franc quickly in
a new defensive position. Preceding the column within sight
were the solo motorcyclists, acting as scouts.

My captain decided to give me one of the two tanks to command. I was ordered to stay till the last in Bourneville—until
10:00 o'clock in the morning, with the Groupe Franc leaving
at 9:30. I waited near the east entrance of the village—the

Germans were expected to come from the east—near the crossroad of the main east-west and north-south roads, so that I could move my tank quickly in any direction.

On the road leading to the east, we had built a stout roadblock by digging holes in the asphalt road, and then sticking thick logs vertically in the holes. We had found this work half completed by some previous unit, with logs all cut and ready to be placed, and we had had time to finish it. The roadblock was of the staggered barricade type, to permit the traffic to flow through it. But at night, or if the enemy came in sight, the barricade could be closed by movable obstacles, such as abandoned vehicles and sliding beams. Just beyond this barricade the road turned to the right in a curve. An antitank gun had been defending this barricade but was now retreating with the main column. There were similar barricades on the roads leading south and north. We left them all open so that I could pass through them with my tank and attack the enemy if he came in sight.

At 10:00 o'clock sharp, just as I was preparing to leave Bourneville with the tank, a German armored car drove suddenly into sight on the road from the east, stopped dead in front of the barricade, apparently saw my tank, and began to move back, in reverse. It was not more than 150 yards away, and I fired and got a hit on it before it could get back around the curve in the road. This was probably the point, I thought, of a whole armored-car platoon. And so I also said to myself, "Let's go!" I then took my tank slowly out through the barricade, firing once more at the armored car without stopping, but hitting it again. It hadn't fired a single shot at my tank. It didn't have time to.

We now went out on the road beyond the disabled armored car and moved on around the curve of the road. And there a second car was heading toward the village to help the other. This was too good. I had nothing to fear, anyway, as I knew the 20-mm. antitank gun on the enemy armored car could not pierce my armor. It was much like a battleship fighting a light cruiser. The moment this new German saw me he headed toward a side road to escape my fire. He opened fire himself, and a direct hit clanked on our armor but didn't come through. I had been right in feeling safe. After firing twice myself this second armored car was out of business. Several enemy motorcyclists following it had pulled off to the left of the road and were firing at me with their machine guns— probably with armor-piercing bullets. Several of them hit the tank but didn't penetrate either. I continued on toward these motorcyclists leaving the road to do so, and now firing high-explosive shells. I know I got several of them.

I headed back on to the road but couldn't see any other enemy cars or troops. The rest of the armored-car platoon had probably decided to pull back—the proper tactics for lightly armored vehicles in the face of a medium tank. I decided not to follow for fear of an ambush. It was well past 10:00 o'clock now, and I had orders to stay only till 10:00. And so I headed back to the village, passing the two disabled armored cars and firing one good shot at each of them. It was probably pure waste and child's play, but it made me feel good. All things considered, I had nothing to brag about. Anyone in a medium tank could have destroyed those two armored cars. But I don't think I would have been able to destroy them at all if the enemy platoon commander had sent his motorcyclists out ahead to reconnoiter the village. I would probably have got one or two of his motorcycle scouts but nobody else. His armored cars would have had time to take cover.

Before leaving Bourneville I had my gunner and my driver close the barricades. I stayed in the tank covering them, ready to shoot, for by now the Germans were probably preparing an attack on the village. I had had a chance to fulfill my mission of slowing down the German reconnaissance elements and thus give the Groupe Franc more time to prepare its defense behind the Risle River. This made me feel a little better than I had for several days. I had made up a little for my poor marksmanship in our Battle of Rouen.

When I arrived in Campigny, I found our two antitank guns already in position in the village, and roadblocks half completed. My captain decided to turn the tank to its noncommissioned officer who was in good shape again. But I must have been bad luck for any tank I touched. The tank commander had been killed in my tank the very morning he took charge of it again. This time the noncommissioned officer of the tank was killed the next day, by a bomb from a Stuka which penetrated his turret.

In Campigny my captain had installed the headquarters of the Groupe Franc in a small castle, situated in the middle of a big park in which all the vehicles had been well concealed and camouflaged under the trees. For the first time in several days I now found the time to shave and wash my hands and face. In the afternoon I went around the village, supervising the work done on roadblocks, and on the antitank-gun and machine-gun emplacements. We had ordered all refugees out of the village.

At 3:00 o'clock I was sent in my sidecar to division headquarters, which had not given any orders since we had arrived in Campigny. I found the headquarters at Carsix, thirty miles to the south in a castle! The staff was standing around big maps, planning the withdrawal of the division to a new position. The Groupe Franc was again to be the last to move.

Shortly after I got back to Campigny, several enemy bombers came over. I was in the middle of the town and there was no time to seek cover in the woods that lay around the village. So I decided to go into the cellar of the nearest house. I found there one of my noncommissioned officers, a placid fellow who never seemed to be bothered by anything. He hadn't shaved for a week, and now having some time to think about it, he went upstairs in the house, hunted around, and came back down in a few minutes with an old square mirror, an old blade and razor, and some soap. He hung the mirror on a nail and began shaving. By then the bombs were coming down, with attack apparently centered on the park and our vehicles. Some more good fifth columnist information, I thought. But now the bombs were coming much nearer. It was funny to watch my noncom trying to shave. He had kept his helmet on as a precautionary measure. Every time a bomb fell a little nearer, his mirror swung on its nail, and plaster fell from the ceiling. But he kept on shaving unperturbed until a terrific crash came and I thought for one moment it was the end of things for us both. Plaster came pouring down covering us. A part of the ceiling above us broke. But the hit was not quite direct and we were still safe even though the house above had been partly destroyed. My noncom, with razor still in his right hand, was now white with plaster. He slowly turned toward me and said very calmly, "The only trouble with this damn war is you can't even shave in peace!"

The planes dropped a few more bombs and left. They had destroyed many houses in the village. I now headed toward the park and saw that two of our trucks were demolished. One was a gasoline truck and the men were busy keeping the flames from spreading. On the outskirts of the village one of our antitank guns had also been destroyed and some of its crew killed. Decidedly our Groupe Franc was getting smaller and smaller with each day.

Next morning, June 15th, we got the order to withdraw once more, this time about sixty miles to the south, to Argentan. But before our Groupe Franc left, it must blow up the two bridges on the Risle: one at St.-Paul-sur-Risle, the other at Pont Audemer. Our tanks, armored cars, and side-car motorcycles had been patrolling along the south bank of the river all the preceding afternoon, but had seen no Germans. The enemy was, however, expected any minute. Our movement to the south had been ordered because the French Army was expected to make its next big stand along the Loire River.

The order to blow the two bridges was a perfect example of an impossible task. If even one staff officer from headquarters had visited the Groupe Franc since it left Rouen, the division commander would have known that we had no explosives. And so my captain sent a motorcycle scout back to tell them that we would have to be given some explosives if we were to do the job. We did have several tank mines and a few *petards de cavalerie*, but it would take a good deal more to blow two bridges. The messenger came back an hour later to report that headquarters had already gone.

We had to do something. For the protection of our Groupe Franc itself, we couldn't leave the bridges merely with a barricade on each side, especially since our tanks and armored cars would have to leave with our column in order to protect it on the march.

The captain decided to leave me behind with a sergeant and four men, and three sidecar motorcycles to blow one bridge, and gave the lieutenant commanding the antitank guns the job of blowing the other; he had one truck and a few men. But first we had to find something to do it with. Together we hunted all along the Risle for some TNT left behind by some French unit in its hasty retreat. And we finally did find a few blocks in an abandoned British depot, but not as many as we needed. To our surprise, the supply depot seemed mainly full of British cigarettes in big wooden boxes, hundreds of them. We decided that a few thousand cigarettes were practically as important as TNT, in view of the boost they would give to the morale of our whole Groupe Franc. And so we left our truck there with two men to pack it full.

I then went on to Pont Audemer with my three sidecars and half of the explosives, and the other lieutenant took his half to the bridge at St.-Paul-sur-Risle, only a few hundred yards from the British depot. I found Pont Audemer completely deserted. It had been bombed and many buildings destroyed. All stores had been looted, all shop windows broken. Arriving at the river where it passes through the northern part of the town, I found that "the bridge" of Pont Audemer was for all practical purposes three bridges!

True, one of them was nothing more than a small wooden lock to regulate the flow of the river, too small for vehicles though troops could easily walk across it. And the middle bridge was no real bridge either, but simply a big building built across the river, which was very narrow at this point. The building served as the marketplace for the town. At both ends of this "bridge," French troops had piled sandbags and anchored them with cement. The floor of the building wasn't strong enough, it seemed to me, to bear the weight of a tank. A light armored car might cross without going through the flooring into the river, but I had my doubts. But enemy motorcycles and passenger cars could use it easily enough provided the sandbags were cleared away first which would be quite a job to do by hand, but could easily be done with one or two blocks of TNT.

I simply didn't have enough explosive to blow this so-called bridge and the regular stone bridge where the main road crossed the river. I therefore decided to concentrate on the main bridge. At both ends of this bridge the French had also built sandbag barricades. My men began to dig a big hole in the middle of the bridge into the heavy pavements, working as fast as they could.

Meanwhile, with my driver, I reconnoitered what to do if we were surprised by a German column. I decided to put the three sidecars in the first side street to the right from the bridge, where they were protected by the buildings from machine-gun fire. We could get in them, and then take another street to the left out of town and be out of German fire because of the cover given by a big building on the other side of the river. In this way we could hit the main road again a few hundred yards to the south. There a stretch of some fifty yards would be dangerous because it would be under direct machine-gun fire from the bridge, but this was a distance so short I thought we could cover it without casualties. I went back to the bridge. The hole was getting bigger and deeper.

Just at that moment we could hear an explosion off a few miles to the east. The antitank lieutenant had blown the other bridge. I then told my men they had dug deep enough and had them put the dynamite in the hole and cover it over. It seemed to me time to act fast and everybody helped. We put some big paving blocks on top, and covered the hole with tightly compressed soil. Then I had my men leave the bridge and wait behind the sandbags. I started off the bridge myself, unrolling the wire that connected the detonator to the TNT. Just as I was climbing over the sandbags at the French end of the bridge, I heard the noise of a motor. A German armored car was coming around the curve of the road just north of the bridge, and it at once began firing at us. I had just the time to jump over the sandbags and throw myself flat. We had no machine guns or any weapon to do much good. The men behind the sandbags opened fire at the armored car with their rifles, using armor- piercing ammunition. We had to blow the bridge fast, now, if at all. As I connected the cord with the detonator, the sandbags gave excellent protection from the fire of the German car. Finally I was able to light the wick leading to the detonator. We then had exactly ninety

seconds to get out before the bridge would go up. I lined the
men behind the sandbags and at a signal from my hand we
leaped toward the little side street to the right all together at
highest speed. We made the side street fifty yards away in
about five seconds—I'm sure it was a record. The German
gunner, surprised by this unexpected action, didn't hit any
of us, we were so fast. In the side street we kept close to the
walls of the houses on the north side of the street. A few seconds later up went the bridge but none of its pieces hit us as
they fell because we were protected by the houses. Arriving
at the dangerous spot on our route, I lined the three sidecars
up and we dashed over it all together, instead of one after
the other. The German fire missed us again. We heard some
bullets whistle, though.

When we finally reached Campigny our rallying point, I
found the other lieutenant there waiting for me. He told me
he had just blown his own bridge and was heading back to
the British depot across the fields, when German motorcyclists appeared on the north bank and fired at him and his
men, but by leaps and bounds they reached the depot. His
men had kept their truck on the safe side of the building and
were still loading cigarettes, even though the door was on
the north side and they had to carry the boxes around under
fire. The truck left the depot under long-range German fire
but nobody was hit. I looked in the truck. The lieutenant told
me there were approximately 350,000 cigarettes. That made
at least 3,000 cigarettes per man for our Groupe Franc. What
a capture!

IV: Retreat to the South

After we blew the bridges on the Risle River on June 15th, we headed full speed south to rejoin our column, and we found it just above Lisieux. Our two armored cars and our tank were acting as the rear guard of our little column, and we found the column halted by a terrific traffic jam in Lisieux itself.

Every little while Nazi bombers came over and machine-gunned the town, and naturally this didn't help any to solve the traffic problem. The bombs seemed mainly to hit refugees rather than troops, particularly women and children, simply because these people did not take cover fast enough. As our column advanced slowly through the town, every time the German planes came at us with machine guns I simply ran into the nearest house, the sturdy stones of which gave me adequate protection against the German bullets. By now we were not firing any more at planes with our machine guns because the results of such fire had been too disappointing.

After we crawled through Lisieux, in accordance with orders received from the division headquarters, we let all the other vehicles pass, and then became the rear guard of the column ourselves, with our remaining motorcycle troops, of which I now had command since the motorcycle-platoon commander had been wounded at Bourgtheroulde the day before. And all day on June 15th we retreated slowly, and closely behind us were the advance elements of the German panzers. We wondered where and how they had crossed the Risle so quickly with their armored cars.

Several times the one medium tank we had left and our armored cars came to grips with them. My motorcycle detachment stayed with the armored cars, in that rear-guard echelon. The Germans would only harass us by shooting and then running. Not once did they try to attack our small column, or even take us from the flanks.

Our tanks always counterattacked boldly, and it put several armored cars out of action. The one thing we really didn't like was the 88-mm. artillery which followed close behind the enemy advance and shelled us every time we halted for as long as an hour.

These small actions were simply incidents, except perhaps for one in which I thought we would certainly lose one of our two remaining armored cars. The road had descended to the bottom of a steep ravine with woods on both sides. In the bottom of this valley, a German 150-mm. shell struck the stone bridge across the stream and made a great hole in it. At the moment, the two armored cars at the rear of the column had not yet crossed the bridge and were busy answering the fire of enemy motorcyclists in the edges of the woods farther back on both sides of the road. Other enemy troops had left their vehicles and were advancing slowly by short rushes along the road. The machine guns of my own motorcycle platoon were adding their return fire from positions taken up along the road between our tank and our armored cars.

The first armored car didn't make it around the hole and slid into it and tipped up at a high angle.

The crew inside the car kept the wheels spinning but to no avail. It seemed plain enough that we could consider the car and its crew both lost. German 77's or 88's began to shell us about that time and we were getting plenty of machine-gun fire in the bargain.

But perhaps there was a way to get out of the jam. I signaled to the medium-tank driver to go back and attack the enemy along both sides of the road, and he headed to the rear to cover the work of rescue. Then the other armored car headed toward the bridge and stopped near it while its commander got out and crawled out on the bridge under fire to hook his car to the one in the hole.

The enemy were still firing, but with less intensity, for our tank was letting them have it with shells from its gun, and my platoon was supporting it with its own machine-gun fire. The armored-car commander got safely back to his car and began to try to pull the other car out of the hole. But his engine simply stalled again and again. Not enough power.

Next the tank came hurriedly back, and the tank commander hooked onto the free armored car, the tank still covering its operation with its own fire. Both vehicles finally pulled the third one out of its hole, and then, with great care, made their way around it. Hardly a minute afterward an 88-mm. shell brought the bridge down entirely.

We arrived in Argentan by evening on June 15th, and immediately moved east of that town to the Forêt de Gouffern, where we took up another defensive position, working all night to prepare roadblocks and a good position for our last antitank gun. The place was extremely well-suited to anti-tank defense. This time we did not set our defense up behind a stream. From Trun, a little town about six miles north of Argentan, to Argentan itself, the main road lay straight across a plateau. This whole plateau was perfectly open without a single tree. Argentan itself, however, lay in a depression, and on both sides of it were thick forests on ground somewhat higher than the plateau.

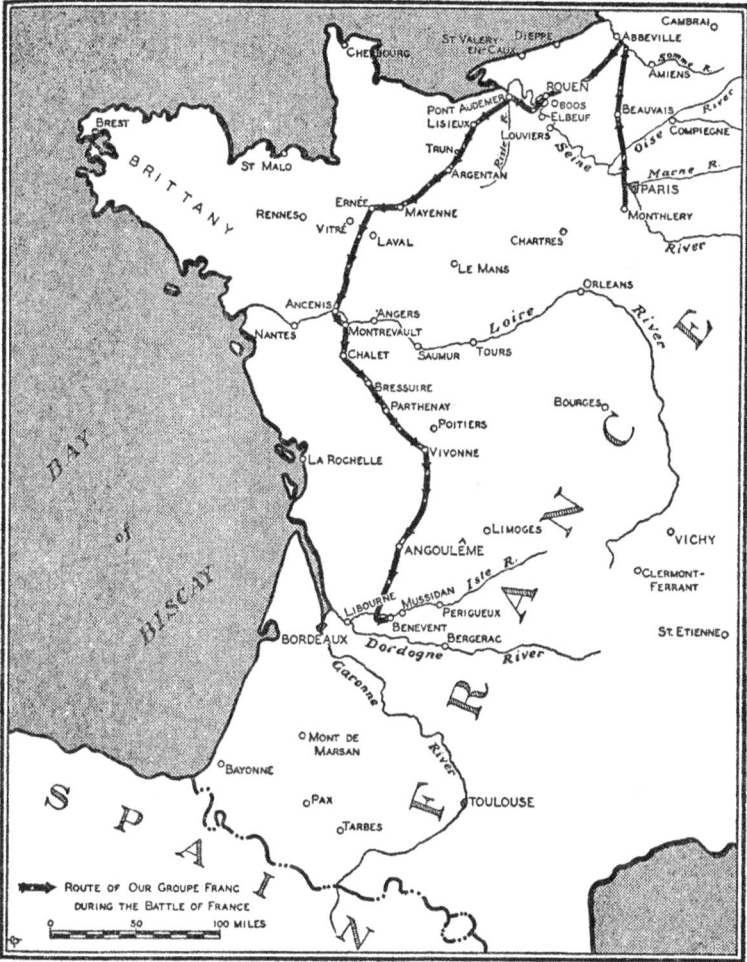

Map 7: Retreat to the south

Our antitank unit was assigned the forest on the east, from the edge of which we could see the entire barren stretch of land for the whole six miles to Trun. The thick woods gave us protection against mechanized attacks, and our antitank gun could be placed to do a marvelous job of destruction. Any tank that rolled across the plateau would be under its direct fire, and could not hope to find any ground whatever which would give it a defiladed position to fire from. On the main road into Argentan, an artillery unit had emplaced two 47-mm. antitank guns and a battery of 75's. To the west of Argentan another artillery unit had another antitank gun in position. A few miles south of the town the artillery of the division was in position, ready to open with concentrations on the plateau. The rest of the division was farther to the south in bivouac.

On the morning of June 16th, it seemed as if the division could make a real stand in this new position, with some chance of repulsing any mechanized attack, surely for a while. The divisional artillery had prepared a heavy barrage to fall on the plateau several hundred yards ahead of our position along the woods. The headquarters and vehicles of the Groupe Franc were south of the forest in the village of Uron in a big estate, where there was security for them.

All day of June 16th we waited for the enemy to show up. But strangely he did not. The Germans always seemed to be well informed to where we were prepared to make a real stand and preferred not to attack, but to wait for the order to retreat to be given the French forces because somewhere else, at a weaker point, a breakthrough had succeeded. Then, as soon as we were on the move again, they would advance and harass us. They knew that our lack of tanks and armored cars would make our column vulnerable during any rearward movement.

At 3:30 on the morning of June 17th we received an order to retreat toward Mayenne and install ourselves near Ernée. This meant a backward jump of sixty miles to the southwest. And again our Groupe Franc was to be the rear guard for the entire column. It was only an hour after we began our withdrawal that the enemy came up again and gained direct contact with light reconnaissance elements. They did not press us hard, however, but kept continuous contact, probably to keep their German High Command informed as to where our column was heading.

Our retreat was slow, around ten miles per hour, and it was interrupted by halts from time to time from traffic jams farther to the south. All the men of the Groupe were completely exhausted, but we had to keep going just the same or be taken by the enemy. One of our armored cars developed motor trouble, which our own mechanics could not fix. The division we were covering was an infantry division and it had neither the time nor the equipment to effect the major repair that was needed. But we decided not to abandon the vehicle, as it had a 25-mm. antitank gun mounted in its turret, a weapon vital to the move. And so one armored car towed the other. This seriously limited mobility, but it was the only way. And it nearly lost us both vehicles.

The two armored cars had been given the mission of staying at the entrance of a village to cover the column as its rearmost elements. The sergeant commanding the towed car left his vehicle to go forward into the village, hoping to find there some bread for his men. The men of the crew stayed inside the car, half sleeping, overcome by the cumulative fatigue of days of fighting.

Suddenly one German motorized infantry vehicle followed by some motorcycle troops came in sight on the road. They saw our French armored cars, halted at the edge of the village, and stopped to observe them. But, seeing no signs of life, they came cautiously right on up almost to the armored cars. Then apparently, deciding to investigate, the enemy infantrymen in the truck jumped out of it into the ditches along the road.

Just then somebody inside one of our armored cars set up a shout, "The Boches are coming!" This woke up everybody dozing, a machine gun of one car went at once into action, and the commander of the other opened with his 25-mm. gun.

Next the German motorcyclists plunged into the ditches, but not before several were casualties from our heavy machine-gun fire. The enemy infantry, however, already in the cover of the ditches, opened fire at almost point-blank range with their antitank rifle, and sent several shots through the armor of the cars, seriously wounding the back driver of the towed car. In the other car, the towing vehicle, the commander was slightly wounded at the right shoulder but continued firing his gun. His back driver was seriously wounded. The commander of the towing car decided it was time to retreat. Because of the noise of the battle, however, he was unable to warn the other vehicle what he was going to do.

He decided to try just the same. His driver stalled his engine several times, but at last got away, but only by breaking the towing cable between the two cars. This car now retreated full speed toward the village, but just as it reached the top of an arched stone bridge at the entrance to the village, it hesitated, and then slowly slipped back down the slope of the bridge and hit the stone railing. The front driver had received a wound this time, but not a serious one. But the car stayed where it was on the bridge.

The other armored car, of course, could not move. The Germans, seeing that it stayed where it was, stopped firing. Cautiously the front driver of this car raised the top of his turret from the inside and peeked out. Then he stepped out of the car with his wounded comrade over his shoulder, and carried him to the near-by enemy troops. A German noncom disarmed him and bawled him out in German for something, he didn't know what. The enemy troops, however, took the wounded French driver to a first-aid station not far back and the other driver followed. He helped dress the wound, but watched constantly for any chance of escaping. A moment came when all the Germans were busy, and he dashed to a near-by house, locking the door behind him. While the Germans were forcing the door, he ran out the back and into the fields behind, rejoining the Groupe Franc that same evening, pale, dirty, and exhausted.

But as the driver with his comrade on his shoulders had headed for the enemy first-aid station, the last tank of our Groupe Franc, whose crew had heard the firing, came tearing out from the village and began firing at the enemy wherever he could be seen. The enemy returned the fire, but the tank commander, when he reached a point near the seemingly abandoned armored car on the bridge, got out of his tank and crawled to the car to find out just what had happened. The wounded front driver inside waved his hand to show that at least some of the crew were still alive.

The tank commander now dragged the wounded out of the car and brought them to the rear, all the time under the fire of the enemy. Then he went back to his tank, and with it pushed the armored car out, away from the stone rail of the bridge.

About that time the commander of the armored car now in German hands came back out of the village with his arms full of bread. He saw the situation at once, crawled toward the armored car on the bridge, started the engine and drove the car back to the village. As he did so, the tank commander attacked straight toward the enemy with his tank and killed several of them. One armored car was lost, but the other saved. We still had one tank and one car. Our retreat continued.

Just before we reached Carrouges, a town halfway between Argentan and Mayenne, our column received a sudden air attack. We caught sight of the planes, five Stukas, only at the last moment, and my captain and I had just time to jump from our command car and into the ditch. They bombed us first and then, apparently because they noticed that our troops had taken cover in the ditches along the sides of the road, came back at us with their machine guns. My captain and I and those near us escaped the fire entirely, however, simply because we were on the curve of the road. The enemy flyers, following the road as they machine-gunned our men, couldn't turn to the right as sharply as the road. A couple of hundred yards beyond the curve the planes had swung in again over the road. Thus every vehicle within the curve was untouched, but the others took something of a beating. And our supply truck was set on fire and destroyed. My trunk locker was in that truck, and now I had nothing left except what I had on. But far worse, our last antitank gun was smashed by a direct bomb hit. And altogether there were a number of casualties.

These were not to be our only serious losses on that day. In the afternoon just after we passed through Mayenne, we had to abandon and blow up our tank. All during the day the oil in the transmission had been heating up so much that smoke could be seen coming out of the tank. And it was so hot inside the tank that it was no longer possible to stay in it. The tank commander was even afraid that his 47-mm. shells might explode because of the heat. But I didn't think there was anything to worry about as far as that was concerned, though it was a fact that the shells were so hot you could hardly touch them with your hand! Finally things got so bad that the tank couldn't keep up with the column any more. And so we salvaged all we could from it, the gasoline, the antitank-gun sight, and the ammunition, and then blew it up. Our only armored vehicle left now was an armored car.

When the Groupe arrived in Ernée, it was sent from there to a hamlet called La Meule, on a little road six miles to the south of Ernée. For the first time now for days we were to be somewhere behind the front of the division as a reserve. The general had finally decided that our Groupe needed a real rest. At La Meule, the Groupe Franc built four staggered barricades with some abandoned vehicles. It was left open to let the traffic pass but we were ready to close it if the enemy came in sight. We placed one machine gun to defend each barricade and what was left of the motorcycle platoon stayed in the center of the hamlet, together with the armored car, ready to move in any direction.

At 4:00 o'clock on the morning of June 18th we were directed by the division commander to send a patrol out on the road from Ernée to the northeast. The general had received information to the effect that the Germans had already passed Mayenne, and he wanted to be sure. My captain decided to send the armored car reinforced by the motorcycle detachment, and the patrol left at 4:30.

About 5:00 a single German sidecar came speeding toward our unit with two men waving big white flags. The motorcyclists came on through the barricade waving their flags to indicate that they had no intention of firing, and our machine gun covering the barricade stayed silent. Arriving in the middle of the hamlet, the Germans made a U-turn and then stopped. The one in the sidecar said, *"Pas tirer, guerre finie. Francais et Allemands amis."* ("Don't shoot, the war is over. The French and the Germans are friends!") Then, just as suddenly, they dashed away at full speed.

But the moment the motorcycle had passed through the barricade, the machine gunner opened up and mowed them down. This struck me as the wrong thing. The two Nazis had come to our unit alone and had not molested us. And at the moment it struck me as next door to plain butchery to open on their backs as they were leaving. I told the gunner so and asked him what officer had given him the signal to fire. He kept silent while I bawled him out, and then simply said that his fingers were itching too much when he saw the two Germans pass squarely into his line of fire. Then the captain arrived, and he admitted that the gunner's action was not exactly sporting, but said that at least the Germans would never be able to report that a French motorized unit was on this little road. Besides their machine was unharmed and this gave us one more badly needed motorcycle for transportation. We also found a submachine gun in the sidecar.

I was wrong. It wasn't till later that I learned how this "don't shoot-the-war-is-over" business had been used extensively by the German Army that day to advance in many places through the French Army without having to fire a shot. The war was not over yet, but there had already been rumors that old Marshal Pétain had asked for an armistice.

A few minutes after we killed the German motorcyclists one of the privates from the motorcycle detachment came back wounded in the shoulder so badly he could hardly talk. But he managed to say, after a drink of brandy, that the Germans were coming, they were practically in Ernée then, on the main road. His patrol had been annihilated, he said, and he was the only man who had escaped the enemy fire.

A short while before, we had sent our gasoline truck to Juvigny, the supply center, about seven miles west of La Meule. It was now 5:15 and it hadn't come back. This was cause enough for worry. The captain decided to send two scouts on motorcycles, one to go east to division headquarters in Chailland and report what had happened; the other to head for Juvigny, and find out what had happened to the truck. In fifteen minutes the first scout was back. It was impossible to

get to division headquarters, for a German column was on
the road a few miles east that lay between us and Chailland.
The column was a mechanized one and was heading toward
the southwest. But we hadn't heard any firing from the troops
of the infantry division. Probably, the "don't-shoot-the-war-
is-over" system was working in that direction.

A few minutes later the other scout came back. The gasoline truck must have been captured, he said. There was an
endless German column rolling south through Juvigny.

So there we were between two enemy columns, one to the
east and the other to the west. We hadn't the strength to
tackle such columns now. "If I only had one or two tanks,"
said my captain. "We could bring enough confusion in one of
the columns to get our vehicles through it." But we had no
tank, no armored car. Only a few trucks, and a few sidecars
and solo motorcycles, with not more than fifty men. Things
seemed hopeless and the war was a matter of days. But we
felt less ready than ever to be taken prisoners.

Perhaps the road to the south was still open. Perhaps if
we kept always between the two enemy columns we might go
faster than they did, and get out ahead of them and away. So
a scout was sent to Bourgneuf, a small village about six miles
to the south, but he soon came back. There was another column going through Bourgneuf, heading right to the west in
the direction of Vitré, Rennes and Brittany. We were closed
in on three sides. The north side was out, unless we wanted
to head straight for the main German forces.

There were two things left. We could either hide in the
woods and hope the enemy wouldn't find us until an armistice became effective, or we could try to get through one of
the German columns and rejoin the French forces. Since we
weren't at all certain how long it might be until an armistice
would be signed, and since we had little chance of staying
undiscovered by the bulk of the German Army for any length

of time, all officers of the Groupe Franc were of the opinion that we should try to get through, whatever might happen.

The Groupe was quickly put in order of march with the solo motorcycles in front, followed by the few sidecars, then the command car for my captain and I, and finally the trucks. At first we headed toward Juvigny. In a sidecar, my captain and I made a rapid reconnaissance to the front of the column. At the last curve of the road before it went into Juvigny we stopped at the top of a little hill to observe. The enemy column was still there, moving rapidly toward the south, apparently with the traffic control well organized. At one curve of the road a German soldier was indicating the right direction to the column by using a small white disc with a handle. Every vehicle also had such a disc, and they were used to change speed or distances, and for other signals. We could see one tank there in Juvigny guarding the crossroad on which our Groupe Franc was advancing, protecting the flanks of the German column. It was a medium tank with its 77-mm. gun pointing right in our direction, and we could see it clearly through our field glasses about 400 yards away. It was very close to the column. Time must have been essential for the German tank didn't even bother to travel the 400 yards in order to post itself at the top of our little hill, a point from which it could have had a much better view.

We had no chance of surprising the German column here against a good tank. My captain therefore decided to try it somewhere else. He ordered the column to make a U-turn and head back toward La Meule, which it did undetected. If the enemy tank had been better posted it could have destroyed us.

We figured now that the Germans were probably posting one tank at each important road crossing. My captain and I accordingly left the Groupe Franc again, after hiding it in a woods, and went to find a crossroads small enough for the

Germans not to expect an attack from it—one where there was no tank on guard. Our map showed a small trail leading south, which cut through the big east-west road at the south base of the triangle formed by the three German columns surrounding us. This would be just the thing, for we would be able to head for the south if our breakthrough was successful.

We found the little dirt road and reconnoitered it, and here again a small hill prevented the enemy from seeing a long stretch of the dirt road near the road on which the enemy column was moving. In fact, this time the terrain was even better than at Juvigny. The hill lay very close to the main road, and from a point just behind its top, only 150 yards from the German column, we were unseen. And there was no German tank.

My captain and I came back to the place where our column was under cover, and led it forward over the narrow track. Some of the trucks had trouble at places where the trail was overly narrow, but we finally got every vehicle up near the main road on which the German vehicles were heading toward the west. We ran the vehicles into the woods that lay on both sides of the trail and camouflaged them so that any German motorcyclist who happened to make a rapid reconnaissance toward us wouldn't see them. But we spotted the vehicles near enough to the trail to hit it quickly when the order to advance was given.

Our idea was to cross through the enemy column without firing a single shot. We figured and hoped that, in such a long column, there would be at least one or two gaps in the flow of traffic long enough in time to enable our column to pass. To signal back when such an interruption began, we sent a volunteer scout crawling toward the road where the Germans were passing. He managed to crawl up to a point only five yards or so from the column, using bushes, weeds, and irregularities of the ground for cover. He had with him four white handkerchiefs knotted together and was to wave this improvised flag as soon as he saw a break in the column.

From 8:00 in the morning on we watched the column anxiously and, so it seemed, endlessly. There must have been at least the equivalent of a whole panzer division passing along that road. Several hundred tanks passed by and thousands of motor vehicles containing infantry. We could see that the march discipline of the column was excellent. Distances appeared to be rigidly kept to lessen the effects of a possible air attack. The enemy seemed, however, to be disregarding all flank protection. They probably knew by this time that our French forces had lost practically all their tanks and anti-tank guns which, of course, were the only real threats to the security of such a column. We knew that rifles and machine guns by themselves had no chance here, so we kept quiet all day long without firing a single shot. We could, of course, have picked off a few of the enemy, but this would only have revealed our presence, and then it wouldn't have taken long for a detachment from the strong column to clean us up.

With my field glasses, lying flat on the grass, I could see every detail of the enemy column. After observing at some length, it seemed to me that what was passing was probably a task force. I saw that all the tanks, the motorcycle units, the artillery guns and engineer vehicles, and the motorized infantry vehicles, were not advancing as organic units. There was instead a succession of small groups or teams, each including several tanks, motorcycles, guns, truckloads of infantry, and supply trucks. Gasoline trucks often traveled between two tanks, but sometimes between two other vehicles. I had a fast glimpse of 105-mm. gun howitzers on self-propelled mounts, each with a big shield of armor in front to protect the crew. I saw the boats of the engineers, and also their flamethrowers. A number of the vehicles had markings painted on their sides, probably for identification of the units. Some of the trucks and motorized infantry vehicles had bright-colored red or yellow cloth over their radiators, probably so they could be identified by their own planes from the air.

The men themselves appeared to be well disciplined, sitting erect in their vehicles, their uniforms in good condition, looking fresh and clean and rested. It was certainly a striking contrast to the unshaven, dirty, and exhausted men in what I had seen of some of our French columns, with little or no traffic discipline and sometimes individual drivers trying to pass each other's vehicles in order to retreat faster to the south. The enemy column was fresh, of course; but it showed the difference between a disciplined, trained, and winning army, and a poorly disciplined and beaten army. More than any other time in my combat experience it struck me forcibly, as I lay there watching the enemy column advancing with precision and order, how greatly the French and the British had underestimated the strength of our Nazi enemies.

The column kept passing, without a single interruption. About noon a few of the enemy stopped along the road and got some water in a farm a hundred yards or so from us, but still we remained unseen.

At last, about 4:00 o'clock of the long day of watching, our scout signalled back with his handkerchiefs that there was a break in the column. We jumped in our vehicles. My captain and I were leading the Groupe Franc in our command car, with the others following behind us. And we stepped on the gas and cleared the main road not more than a few hundred yards behind the rear of the long German column. As we tore across the road, I had a quick glance of German tanks coming up from the other way in the distance. And suddenly I could hear tanks firing somewhere not far off. We raced ahead. But only the first half of our column gained the other side of the main road. The other half was caught and completely smashed by the fire of the oncoming enemy tanks.

The rest of us kept on at full speed toward the south thinking we would be pursued. But the enemy didn't give chase. Our unit was too small to interest them, and they kept to their main objective, heading farther into French territory.

We sped on for a few miles and then slowed down. My captain now sent out three solo motorcycles as a point. We followed right behind them in our command car which we now called our "tank" because we had installed a machine gun on its top. The five sidecars that had managed to break through free we used to make short but continual reconnaissance out to our flanks. The three trucks left in the Groupe followed right behind my captain's car. In all we had now only some twenty-five men, with four machine guns and our rifles. Our ammunition truck, supply truck, kitchen truck, gasoline truck, all had been lost.

As we neared the village of St. Pierre la Cour, I suddenly saw the three motorcyclists jumped from their machines into the ditches by the road. At the same time we could hear firing very close ahead. My captain and I dived into the ditch from our car and a moment later a volley of machine-gun bullets hit the front of it shattering our windshield. We tried raising our heads a bit to see something, but at once bullets would whiz past our heads and make us duck again.

Meanwhile, however, the three motorcyclists had advanced by crawling to determine the strength of the enemy. Suddenly one of them jumped up on the road and yelled, "We are French, you damned fools!"

The French troops ahead had seen a motorized column advancing on the road with motorcycles and all, and had thought at once that we could be nothing but Germans. And so at least once in my life I had heard French bullets whistling past my ears as businesslike as any others.

This incident made us change the way our unit was advancing along the road. My captain decided to put all the motorcycles and sidecars in the rear of the column. We also took the machine gun off our command car, which without it looked very much like any regular French passenger car, except for its gray-green color. The car now became our point. In this way we hoped that no other French troops would fire at us. They did not, I'm glad to say. But each time we passed or came near a friendly infantry unit in retreat, we acted with particular caution.

The most amazing thing about our escape through the German column was that we met no other enemy forces until we reached the Loire River, late that evening, sixty whole miles farther to the south. The Germans had concentrated their forces on a few roads, thus apparently to slice up the French Army by going from the northeast to the southwest, toward Brittany.

At Ancenis, on the Loire River, the bridge was still standing, but mined, however. Here the handling of the traffic was excellent, and we quickly crossed the Loire, which was very wide at that place. At least, we now hoped, we would see a real organized defense make a good stand behind the Loire. But our hopes soon vanished. For, as behind the Seine, no defensive preparations had been made.

Since our own division, the one we had acted as rear guard for, could probably be considered as lost and surrounded somewhere back around Ernée, it seemed best to find some other division and get ourselves attached to it. For we had lost our kitchen truck and all of our gasoline. Our men could hardly go on fighting long without food, or gasoline for the vehicles. So now, since we had some choice, we searched for some good unit to be attached to. We were fortunate enough to find a splendid commander of a cavalry division, which we knew was an excellent outfit, half motorized and half horse.

This commander was by now, however, almost a general without a division, for his unit had lost by far the greater part of its men and vehicles, and all its animals, in battle in northern France. But the supply trains of the division were left, and an antitank-gun company, and a few artillery pieces—in all some five hundred men. The general had known my captain somewhere before. He decided to use the Groupe Franc as a protection for his headquarters.

We now headed for Montrevault where his headquarters were, a village south of the Loire. There we put our machine guns in position, with one man at each gun, and rotated our men on this duty. And now the entire Groupe Franc went to sleep. For we were more than exhausted, we were practically dead. Before I turned in myself I had a delicious bath in a small stream of water, which I needed for I had not undressed for two weeks. I found no bed anywhere, and so I spread myself out on the grass, under a tree, and there sawed them off from 1:00 in the morning of June 19th to 7:00 in the morning of June 20th. Thirty hours, without eating, without waking! Even then one of the men woke me up to say that the Groupe would be leaving in half an hour. Our men fixed a whale of a breakfast for me, eggs, bread, and all. And I ate it all and felt fine, ready to fight again. My captain, who had also slept a long time, told me that the few men left in the division had been fighting the enemy since early that morning, and had prevented the enemy from crossing the river in that vicinity. But the general had to order a retreat because a German column had been able to cross the Loire somewhere off to the east.

From this morning on, until the night of June 24th, four days later, we saw no enemy, except numerous hostile planes over our heads. We kept going at full speed to the south, through Bressuire, Parthenay, Poitiers, Angoulême. Near Parthenay, in Glazier, a little village, we heard Pétain on the radio publicly telling the people of France that he had asked for an armistice.

Near Poitiers, in the village of Laverre, we organized a position behind a tiny river, called the Clain. All day on the 22d we stayed there waiting for the Boche to show up. We still had a faint hope: someone remembered that Nostradamus in his prophecies had said that France would be invaded from three sides, but that the Germans would finally be beaten near Poitiers. Here we were near Poitiers, but the big battle prophesied so many centuries ago was not forthcoming. Instead, there was another order to retreat, at 2:00 on the morning of June 23d, just before the Germans reached our position. And all during the day of the 23d we retreated slowly, stuck in the middle of a never-ending jam of traffic.

On the 24th, near Angoulême, our repair truck with our mechanics and one truck from the cavalry division were taken prisoner by the advance guard of the German panzer unit we had on our trail. The truck had had motor trouble and had been left behind with the mechanics who tried to make a hasty repair.

In the afternoon of the 24th our Groupe arrived in Benevent, on the south side of the Isle River, a tributary of the Dordogne, a place about sixty miles northeast of Bordeaux. Since we had no more explosives, we were unable to blow the bridge across the Isle. We cut big trees, however, and installed a strong barricade. And antitank guns from the cavalry division were set up to defend it.

About 8:00 o'clock in the evening we saw some enemy troops on the other side. We fired and they fired back. Since it was late and the Germans had probably advanced some distance during the day, my captain figured that they would wait until morning before attempting a crossing. About that time we were informed that the French had blown up all the bridges along the Dordogne, thirty miles to the south. In other words, we were now trapped between two rivers by the action of our own higher command. We therefore prepared to make a last and desperate stand the next morning.

But at 11:00 o'clock that night we heard by radio that the armistice had been finally signed with both Italy and Germany, and that it would become effective in a few hours, at exactly 1:30 in the morning of June 25th.

We still had ammunition, however. And there were Germans on the other side of the stream. If we didn't use it up, we would probably have to surrender it. My captain decided accordingly to fire and fire and fire until exactly 1:30 in the morning. And we fired every kind of ammunition we could find in the division supply trucks: tracer bullets, armor-piercing bullets, regular bullets. The Germans fired back, but not very much. Our antitank guns kept firing toward the enemy with shells. We certainly must have killed a few of the enemy, but on our part we suffered only one casualty. At 1:30 on the dot we stopped. And the Germans stopped too.

Now the silence was overwhelming. In the dark of the night we heard the Germans singing the official Nazi song and hollering "*Seig Heil!*" or "*Nach England*" every once in a while. We answered with the *Marseillaise*, but the seventeen of us left in the Groupe Franc made a sad job of it. The *jour de gloire* had not come, and France had been defeated worse than it had ever been in all its two thousand years of history.

For a few days, and until the demarcation line between the occupied and so-called unoccupied zones was finally marked, we kept on the alert at all times. We kept all our vehicles on the road, toward the southeast, ready to leave at any minute if the enemy showed any sign of crossing the river to occupy our village. Finally we learned that the demarcation line between the two zones was to be twenty kilometers east of the railroad line between Angoulême and Mont de Marsan. This made the line pass only two miles west of our

village. We were, therefore, already in the last village of unoccupied France, the next one being Montpon, on the River
Isle, where the Germans soon sent a detachment.

I stayed on in Benevent until the beginning of August,
supervising the demobilization of our men and helping refugees who crossed the line to go back home into the occupied
territory. I myself was released from the Army on August 8,
1940, and rejoined my wife on the Riveria. After several
months I finally obtained the papers that enabled me to leave
France, but I was unable to cross Spain to Lisbon, without
taking the risk of being put in a Spanish concentration camp.
This was done to many young Frenchmen by the Spanish gov-
ernment, acting under pressure from Berlin. Berlin wanted
to prevent all Frenchmen of military age wanting to join the
British from crossing Spain and Portugal.

And so in desperation I got aboard a small cargo boat
which ran the English blockade across the Mediterranean and
landed in Algeria. From there I took a train to Morocco, and
then to Tangiers opposite Gibraltar, which at that time was
still an international town. From Tangiers I took a plane to
Lisbon, where I met my wife who, as an American citizen,
had been able to cross Spain. And later we both sailed for the
United States. This trip from France back to the United States
seems simple to speak of, but it actually took four months
because of the endless complications. It felt good, I can as-
sure you, to be back in the United States, and free.

Appendix

Composition of Gerard's Tank-Fighter Team

Commander: Captain (in command car with driver).

Second-in-Command: Second lieutenant (Indian sidecar, driver).

Tank Platoon: Second lieutenant. 5 medium tanks, Somua M-39 (2 squads of 2 tanks each, plus 1 command tank). 14 men.

Armored-Car Platoon: Second lieutenant. 5 armored cars, Panhard, M-1939 (2 squads of 2 cars each, plus command car). 19 men.

25-mm. AT Platoon: First lieutenant. Two 25-mm. AT guns; 2 light machine guns; 4 half-tracks. Each squad had 1 AT gun and 2 half-tracks, one being a prime-mover. 1 command car; 1 GMC truck for ammunition. 30 men.

47-mm. AT Platoon: Second lieutenant of FA. Two 47-mm. AT guns; 2 Laffly prime-movers; 2 GMC trucks for personnel; 2 GMC trucks for ammunition; 2 light machine guns; 1 command car. Each squad had 1 AT gun and 1 prime-mover. 34 men.

Heavy MG Platoon, Motorized: Second lieutenant. 6 heavy machine guns; 6 GMC trucks for personnel. 3 squads, each with 2 heavy machine guns and 2 trucks. Plenty of ammunition in trucks. 1 command car. 48 men.

Motorcycle Detachment: Second lieutenant. 1 motorcycle platoon plus 1 additional motorcycle squad. 13 Indian sidecars in the platoon and 5 sidecars in the squad (total, 18). Platoon consisted of 2 squads of 5 sidecars each, plus 1 sidecar for mechanic, 1 sidecar for liaison, and 1 for commander. 6 light machine guns (2 per squad). 35 men.

Headquarters Platoon: Master sergeant. 5 liaison sidecars, 1 detached to each platoon except motorcycle platoon. 10 men (driver and substitute driver per sidecar). 10 solo motorcycles for liaison, transmission of orders, reconnaissance, and observation. These were Royal machines. 10 men. Kitchen truck, 3.5 tons. 6 men (driver, baker, butcher, 3 cooks). Repair and maintenance truck, plus sidecar for liaison. 6 mechanics. Telephone truck, to connect headquarters of Groupe Franc to outposts and regular telephone lines. 6 men. Radio truck plus 1 GMC truck for personnel of telephone and radio sections; two-way radio set. 6 men. 3 gasoline trucks, GMC. 6 men (3 drivers, 3 refuelers). 2 ammunition trucks, GMC (carried AT mines, ammunition for tanks and armored cars, etc). 4 men (including 1 tailor). 1 supply truck, GMC (reserve food and clothing). 4 administrative clerks.

RECAPITULATION

Total strength: 8 officers, 241 enlisted men.

Medium tanks: 5. Armored cars: 5.

47-mm. AT guns: 7 (including those in tanks).

25-mm. AT guns: 7 (including those in armored cars).

Heavy machine guns: 6.

Light machine guns: 20 (including those in armored vehicles).

Command cars: 4.

Sidecars: 25.

Solo motorcycles: 10.

Half-tracks: 4.

Laffly prime-movers: 2.

GMC light trucks: 14.

Heavy-ammunition trucks for 47-mm. AT gun: 2.

Special vehicles: 4 (kitchen, maintenance, telephone, and radio trucks).

Total vehicles: 75.

Appendix
Equipment of Gerard's Tank-Fighter Team

Somua Medium Tank, Model M-39

Weight: 20 tons.

Crew: Driver, gunner, and commander.

Dimensions: Length, 18 feet 7 inches. Height, 9 feet 5 inches.

Climbing ability: 40 degrees.

Armor: 41-mm. (1.6 inches) on thickest part; cast-steel turret in front.

Armament: one 47-mm. AT gun, one 7.5-mm. machine gun.

Ammunition: 120 rounds for 47-mm. gun, 5,000 for M.G.

Engine: V-8, 210 h.p., water-cooled.

Speeds: 5 forward, 1 reverse.

Maximum speed: 29 m.p.h.

Cruising radius: 140 miles.

Communication: W/T radio, flags.

Suspension: 9 bogie wheels, 4 bogies with leaf springing, 1 independent bogie wheel; suspension protected by skirting.

Performance: Step, 2 feet 11 inches. Water forded, 3 feet 3 inches. Trench crossing, 7 feet 10 inches.

Panhard Armored Car, Model 1939

Crew: Front driver, back driver, gunner, and commander.

Wheeled vehicle: 4 x 4, independent wheels, limited to roads and easy terrain.

Armor: 8-mm. (.32 inch), protecting crew against machine-gun armor-piercing bullets at normal distances.

Tires: Bullet-proof.

Maximum speed: 45 to 50 m.p.h.

Armament: one light machine gun, one 25-mm. AT gun.

47-MM. AT Gun, Model 1939 (Schneider)

Muzzle velocity: 2,800 f.s.

Shell: 3.8 pounds.

Ammunition: High-explosive or armor-piercing.

Maximum range: 5,500 yards.

Elevation: 15 degrees.

Depression: 5 degrees.

Traverse: 45 degrees.

Tires: Bullet-proof.

Weight: 2,310 pounds.

Penetration: 60-mm. (2.4 inch) at 30 degrees at 600 yards, 3 inches at 500 yards. 60-mm. (2.4 inch) at 15 degrees at 200 yards.

25-MM. AT Gun, Semiautomatic, Model 1935 (Hotchkiss)

Successfully used against light tanks.

Muzzle velocity: 3,000 f.s.

Shell: .916 pounds.

Ammunition: Either high-explosive or armor-piercing.

Maximum range: 11,200 yards.

Elevation: 15 degrees.

Depression: 5 degrees.

Traverse: 60 degrees.

Weight: 1,050 pounds.

Penetration: 40-mm. (1.6 inch) armor at 30 degrees at 400 yards. 60-mm. (2.4 inch) plate at normal impact at 100 yards.

Sight for all AT Guns

Very clear, wide angle of vision.

Magnification: 4.

Knob to adjust sight for personal vision.

Graduations for range on glass itself.

Graduations on the horizontal hair to facilitate the taking of leads.

Indian Sidecars

Fast, a lot of power. Bathtub had been added to what was normally a solo motorcycle. No place to carry baggage.

Too low. Cross-country performance very poor.

Noisy, fragile (always two or three in repair).

Not economical; low mileage per gallon.

General Motors Trucks, Model ACK

Excellent equipment.

Four wheels; fast and easy to drive.

No motor troubles.

Silhouette too high; difficult to camouflage under trees.

Coachwhip Publications

CoachwhipBooks.com

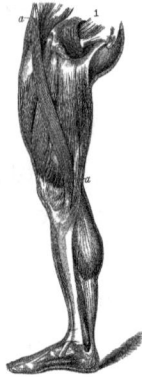

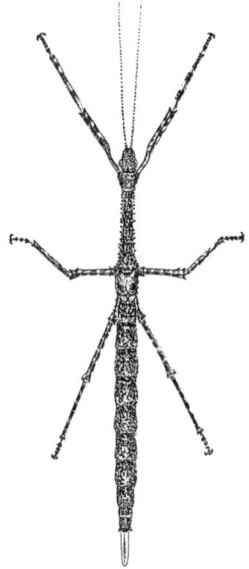

COACHWHIP PUBLICATIONS

ALSO AVAILABLE

TANKS

AND HOW TO DRAW THEM

TERENCE T. CUNEO

ISBN-13 978-1-61646-021-1

www.ingramcontent.com/pod-product-compliance
Lightning Source LLC
Chambersburg PA
CBHW031519040426
42445CB00009B/311